MAKE YOUR OWN

MEDITERRANEAN
GARDEN

MAKE YOUR OWN
MEDITERRANEAN
GARDEN

how to create a sunshine garden –
wherever you are

PATTIE BARRON
FOREWORD BY RICHARD MABEY
PHOTOGRAPHS BY SIMON McBRIDE

aqua marine

For my parents, who first took me to the Med

This edition is published by Aquamarine

Aquamarine is an imprint of Anness Publishing Ltd
Hermes House, 88–89 Blackfriars Road, London SE1 8HA
tel. 020 7401 2077; fax 020 7633 9499
www.aquamarinebooks.com; info@anness.com

© Anness Publishing Ltd 1999, 2003

This edition distributed in the UK by The Manning Partnership
Ltd, 6 The Old Dairy, Melcombe Road, Bath BA2 3LR;
tel. 01225 478 444; fax 01225 478 440;
sales@manning-partnership.co.uk

This edition distributed in the USA and Canada by National
Book Network, 4501 Forbes Boulevard, Suite 200, Lanham,
MD 20706; tel. 301 459 3366; fax 301 429 5746;
www.nbnbooks.com

This edition distributed in Australia by Pan Macmillan
Australia, Level 18, St Martins Tower, 31 Market St, Sydney,
NSW 2000; tel. 1300 135 113; fax 1300 135 103;
customer.service@macmillan.com.au

This edition distributed in New Zealand by David Bateman Ltd,
30 Tarndale Grove, Off Bush Road, Albany, Auckland;
tel. (09) 415 7664; fax (09) 415 8892

A CIP catalogue record for this book is available from the
British Library.

Publisher: JOANNA LORENZ
Managing Editor: HELEN SUDELL
Designer: LISA TAI
Editorial readers: PENELOPE GOODARE AND JOY WOTTON
Production Controller: SARAH TUCKER
Photographer: SIMON MCBRIDE
Stylist: PATTIE BARRON

Previously published as *Create a Mediterranean Garden*
10 9 8 7 6 5 4 3 2 1

Plant Hardiness Notes

The plants described in this book have
been given hardiness ratings to help you
buy plants that will survive in your
garden environment.
Unless otherwise stated, all the
plants prefer a sunny outlook and
well-drained soil.

Key to Symbols

FT (Frost tender) Plant may be damaged
   by temperatures below 5°C/41°F
*   Half hardy: plant can withstand
     temperatures down to 0°C/32°F
**   Frost hardy: plant can withstand
     temperatures down to −5°C/23°F
*** Fully hardy: plant can withstand
     temperatures down to −15°C/5°F

Contents

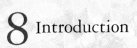

Foreword

Much of what we take for granted in modern gardens started out in the Mediterranean. Fountains and fragrant herbs, poppies, pots on the patio, tulips amongst the rocks. Some of mankind's most ancient and widespread crops – figs, grapes, olives, wheat – were first domesticated in the rich flood plains of Syria and the Holy Land, and historians reckon that this is where the very idea of horticulture was invented 8,000 years ago.

Any gardening gestures towards the Med are homages to this heritage. But for Pattie Barron – and an increasing number of gardeners imprisoned under the grey skies of more northerly regions – they are also a way of conjuring up that real arcadia that Keats called "the warm South": full of "Provençal song and sunburnt mirth". The Mediterranean garden is a refuge of southern light and sensuousness, of terracotta and turquoise, of the savour of thyme and basil, of tomatoes and apricots eaten, if you are a very lucky gardener, under the shade of your own olive tree. Yet ironically, in our increasingly unpredictable climate, it has also become a very practical model of how to garden in conditions of drought. Pattie's first garden was in Bath, a city whose honeyed stone buildings and terraced slopes give it something of the character of a Mediterranean hill town.

Above: *Wildflowers blooming by the roadside in Greece show us how to garden in drought conditions.*

Opposite: *Pattie Barron's terraced Mediterranean garden reflects the luxuriance of southern scrublands.*

It had clumpings and associations prompted by glimpses of the serendipitous way Mediterranean plants grouped themselves in the wild (and I put in my hap'orth of suggestions here): Spanish broom insinuated by honeysuckle and wild peas, dwarf bulbs under conifers, rosemary in full flower against a purple November sky, thymes and spurges trailing over the terrace walls, phlomis by a rock and a pomegranate in a pot – the whole riotous entanglement and repeated alternations of glade and grove reflecting the luxuriance and surprise that makes the southern scrublands so stirring. Pattie's new garden is bigger and flatter, and needs different solutions, all of which are faithfully revealed in this book. To the natural planting schemes, for example, are added more of the ingenious human artefacts of the Mediterranean garden: home-made mosaic tables, inspired by Moorish patterns seen in Portuguese palaces; walls hung with pots of vivid geraniums, as they were in a village in the Corbières hills.

This is a book by a Mediterranean aficionado and well-known gardening writer, who admits she is still learning, and written in her inimitable style, which so perfectly catches the brio and colour and idiosyncrasy of "the warm South". And what helps make it the most practical, the most realistic guide to creating that oasis of sunlight at home is that much of the work on the garden itself, and the illustrations, was done in one of the most infamously gloomy northern summers imaginable.

Richard Mabey

introduction

Making the Mediterranean garden

I have written this book so that others can experience the thrill of making a garden that is as boisterous as it is beautiful; a garden that sizzles with vivid colour and is alive with bees and butterflies; a garden of intoxicating scents that suffuse your skin and make you feel good even if the day is grey. And I also wanted to share the pleasure of a garden that somehow puts itself together with little intervention from the gardener – no planting plans required – and, as a bonus, needs no watering and very little maintenance.

This kind of Mediterranean garden is based not on the grand Riviera gardens, but on the countryside that surrounds them, notably the tough, self-sufficient native plants that colonize scrubby hillside and stony pasture, wasteland and seashore. These plants share one important characteristic: they are drought-resistant, equipped by nature to cope for long periods without water. Thus they are ideal for gardens where rain does not fall for weeks at a time as well as for gardeners who have better ways to spend their time than wielding watering cans and hosepipes.

Many of these Mediterranean natives are aromatic herbs that we are familiar with: rosemary, thyme, bay, fennel, oregano, sage. Although they can be grown in pots around the back door, they find their true rhythm in the garden as handsome flowering evergreen shrubs that can easily be clipped into submission if they grow too exuberantly. Lavender, wormwood, euphorbia, broom and cistus are just a few examples of the signature wild plants of the Mediterranean that have already proved their worth to us on home ground. Many of the bulbs we take for granted – tulips, grape hyacinth, crocus, narcissi – originated on Cretan hillsides, the oak scrub of Greece or the rocky slopes of Spain. Agaves, aloes, palms, eucalyptus and acacias, immigrants that arrived long ago and have settled and spread, are all part of the eclectic Mediterranean flora; incredibly, this region – from Morocco, Portugal and

Left: *To the backdrop of a pink-blossomed Judas tree and pencil cypresses, terracotta pots of plants are lined up to greet the sun in this Provençal garden.*

Right: *Many gardens in the Mediterranean, like this one in Cortona, Italy, are literally carved out of the hillsides, and the terracing offers protection from the wind.*

Spain in the west, to the Lebanon, Israel, Egypt and Libya in the east, taking in southern France, Italy, Greece and the coast of Turkey – boasts well over 10,000 species of flowering plants, with over 6,000 in Greece alone, offering a rich and varied seam for us to plunder.

The popular concept is that Mediterranean plants are tender and delicate, and therefore cannot possibly flourish in anything less than sultry, sunny conditions year round. If that were the case, how could they survive halfway up mountainsides, growing on poor, rocky soil, living without a drop of water for weeks on end? Coastal winds can desiccate plants in the firing line, and cold winters deliver the occasional frost. The native plants of the scrublands – *maquis* and *garrigue* – have learned over the centuries how to survive hardship, throwing out protective sunscreens of aromatic vapour or deflecting the sun's rays with shimmery foliage, storing water in succulent leaves or retaining it with a fine covering of hairs. It is these same characteristics that make them unappealing to pests; their tough constitutions also help them shrug off disease. No gardener could ask for more.

My first garden of Mediterranean native plants, created five years ago, was in a frost pocket, an ideal testing ground. Although the terraces carved out of a grassy slope faced the sun for much of the day, in winter the frost rolled down them, hit the wall and settled threateningly on the lowest terrace. That first winter, the snow covered the garden in a thick blanket, the frost turned the purple sages silver, and I held my breath. What I discovered was that so long as you keep the roots dry and the crowns from rotting, you will have few failures. I also discovered that,

Above: *Native drought-resistant plants in this Provençal garden create an exciting alternative lawn.*

Left: *The hillsides of Umbria, peppered with olives, vines and poppies, provide inspiration for our own gardens.*

given the right conditions, these plants grow gratifyingly fast. And while most new gardens have pockets of unappealing bare earth between developing plants, the Mediterranean garden has swathes of creamy stones, creating satisfying spaces.

In fact it is stones, not endless sunshine, that are the secret of success. Here lies the groundwork: bottomless buckets of grit or gravel to give the soil sharp drainage so that the plants do not languish in wet, compacted ground and rot in the conditions they detest. The soil is not enriched with fertilizer or manure, but texturized with spadefuls of stones that are also layered on top as a water-retaining mulch, which keeps the foliage crowns dry and absorbs heat to benefit the plants. After three summers of severe drought conditions, the drought-proof plants of my Mediterranean garden continued to thrive while the herbaceous borders on the other sides of the walls visibly wilted, lawns turning to a brown crisp.

In sharp contrast, the following summer was one of the wettest on record, but while more conventional gardens were flattened, the Mediterranean garden bounced back, thanks to a combination of the plants' natural resilience and the gravel's rapid drainage.

Given the conditions they thrive on in the wild, these plants make a magical kind of *maquis*, needing no special

planning for their colours and textures to complement one another. As many of the photographs in this book show, most of the pleasing plant partnerships just happen, proving that when wild plants from the same vicinity grow together, they make their own harmonies. Unlike the real thing, this man-made *maquis* grows richer and more ebullient through the summer under a more equable climate than that of the uncompromising Mediterranean. By late summer, there is little to catch the eye in real *maquis* and *garrigue*. The simulated Mediterranean garden, however, is action-packed throughout the year, providing a lively landscape that never rolls over and goes to sleep as most gardens do. The predominant shrubs and subshrubs are evergreen – or evergrey or eversilver – and make pleasing textural shapes that carry the garden through a calmer phase in the colder months. Spring erupts suddenly when the flowering bulbs display their primary-bright livery of red, blue and yellow, and the bark of the

Above: *Olive and cotton lavender in the Mediterranean garden at The Abbey Gardens, Tresco, in the Scilly Isles.*

Left: *The terrace in my garden offers places for pots, and a seat in the sun.*

Above: *The plants in my Mediterranean garden, given the conditions they favoured, filled the terraces within two years. Lavender, cistus, euphorbia and asphodels made their distinctive mark on the terrain.*

Left: *An evocative garden at the Chelsea Flower Show, London, conjures up the spirit and warmth of Provence with a mixture of formal clipped box trees and informal native plants.*

Judas tree is studded with rich pink blossom. In summer the garden is an explosion of foliage and flower: yellow asphodel and pink cistus, mauve iris and steel blue sea holly are just some of the highlights.

Amongst this man-made *maquis*, there is also a place to celebrate the Mediterranean's ancient tradition of growing delectable plants in containers. Citrus originated in Persia, not Provence, but the lemon tree in a terracotta pot has become a compulsory souvenir of the Mediterranean. Even in the smallest container, the brilliant shades of bougainvillea make the biggest splash.

And on the terrace or in the windowbox, pink, scarlet and cerise pelargoniums recall the dazzling whitewashed walls of Greece and pretty green-shuttered houses of the Midi.

Your own starting point for creating a Mediterranean garden might be no more than a small patch of ground or an individual bed. But when you discover the joys of a spirited, sensual garden that keeps delivering surprises as well as scratches, that throws out enticing perfumes as well as pungent aromas, that delights the eye for every month of the year, you will doubtless, like me, soon be looking for more.

Mediterranean plants

Familiarize yourself with the ultimate

garden plants: tough drought-busters

drought-proof

with specially developed mechanisms

refined over the ages that enable them

natural survivors

to survive in the wild, and thrive in

your garden.

garrigue & maquis

Mediterranean plants in the wild

If you want to make a Mediterranean garden, it makes sense to acquire a passing knowledge of the territory that these plants naturally inhabit, so that you can make your garden as hospitable as possible for them. Most of the plants featured in this book grow in Mediterranean *maquis* or *garrigue*, two important types of vegetation which have evolved as a consequence of the degeneration of evergreen forests that used to predominate in the region. Felling trees for fuel, clearing brushwood, forest fires, grazing animals: all have played their part in opening up the forest and letting in light, so that the undergrowth has become more prevalent.

Maquis is usually the first stage in the deterioration of mature forest. It consists of shrubby trees or evergreen shrubs of around 2m/6ft or more that form fairly dense, sometimes impenetrable thickets. Typical *maquis* inhabitants are strawberry tree, dwarf evergreen oak, myrtle, Spanish broom, rosemary, lentisk, juniper and cistus. All are drought-resistant, or they would simply not be able to survive the tough, dry conditions.

Where the *maquis* is grazed, burnt or cut down further and deteriorates into rocky heathland, or where olive groves, pastures or orchards have been abandoned and colonized by wild plants, the resultant vegetation of dwarf evergreen shrubs is called *garrigue*. Although the soil is thin over the limestone rocks and has few nutrients, it supports a broad variety of resilient plants that, unlike the

KNOW YOUR TERRAIN

There is an easy way, according to one botanist, to identify maquis from garrigue: the garrigue bites you on the ankle, the maquis pokes you in the eye!

Above: *The garrigue in flower at the Massif des Maures, Provence.*

Left: Cistus albidus *prospers in the dry, rocky terrain of Italy's Ligurian Alps.*

Above: *In spring, the wildflowers of Greece make a rich tapestry of colour on wasteland and wayside.*

Above: *Although the* garrigue *is full of flowers in late spring, the hot, dry summer soon takes its toll.*

Above: *Brooms, French lavender and cistus flowering profusely in Corsican countryside.*

dense population of the *maquis*, grow more sparsely among the rocks and rarely reach over 50cm/20in in height. These include lavender, phlomis, juniper, euphorbia, herbs such as thyme and rue, perennials, annuals and many bulbs such as tulips, crocuses, irises and grape hyacinth. *Garrigue* is heavily grazed by goats and sheep, which keeps many shrubs stunted, although some plants over the centuries have developed noxious chemicals, aromatic oils or spiny foliage that make them unpalatable. This explains the huge groves of asphodels that thrive on overgrazed land.

The plants of the *maquis* – *macchia* in Italy – and *garrigue* hit their peak early in the year, as you would expect in a climate that is characterized by short, mild, moist winters and long, hot, dry summers. It is the winter rains that sustain the plants and give them enough stamina to endure the summer drought, which can last for over three months. Because of the near absence of cloud and fog, there is a large contrast between daytime and night-time temperatures. In January the daytime temperatures in the Mediterranean region are from about 5–10°C/41–50°F but at night temperatures can fall to freezing and below, so that the occasional frost is not unknown.

Spring is beautiful but brief; most colour comes from the *garrigue*, although the *maquis* has its share of flowers, including yellow broom, pink and white cistus and tree heather. In late spring, after the rains, annual wildflowers spring up on the plains and hillsides, carpeting them with colour. The great burst of flower is soon followed by the parched landscape of summer, although the *maquis* stays predominantly dark green, with thick evergreen leaves equipped to protect the plants from excessive water evaporation. The long, hot days and sun-baked earth slow down plant life to the extent that many plants turn dormant, held in a kind of suspended animation; annuals set seed, while bulbous plants retreat underground.

Autumn is a long season, bringing rain that falls mostly at night, and makes a welcome end to the dry, dusty heat. Many plants start growing, the countryside turns green once more and the season sometimes called "little spring" starts to live up to its nickname. The *garrigue* is filled once more with flowers.

Mediterranean plants in the temperate garden

Given the right conditions, shrubby plants of *maquis* and *garrigue*, as well as some annual wildflowers and seaside plants of the Mediterranean region, will thrive in a more moderate climate. In fewer hours of sun, some plants may not flower so freely – wild sweet peas will not grow in such profusion as they do in Tuscany, and a potted bougainvillea will never romp up the house wall – but they still delight and surprise. What their success in your garden chiefly depends on, however, is giving them the type of terrain they are accustomed to. Free-draining, open-textured soil is crucial. Instead of lacing your soil with manure or fertilizer, stones – or gravel or grit – are the magic ingredient.

Many Mediterranean plants grow on limestone, so it is unfortunately the case that gardens with heavy, acid soils

Above: *In a sunny, sheltered spot, you can grow your own vines and reap a harvest of succulent grapes in autumn.*

Above: Lampranthus *and* Phlomis fruticosa *bask in the summer sunshine.*

Left: *Given the stony, free-draining soil they are used to in the wild, Mediterranean plants will provide a sizzling summer display.*

Above: *As summer progresses, the main flowering season continues with irises, tufted French lavender and sprawling banks of rock roses.*

Left: *In early spring, the Mediterranean garden is at its greenest; euphorbias display their frothy lime green flowerheads, coronilla is constantly in flower while rosemaries blossom in shades of blue, pink and lilac.*

will not produce good results; perhaps the answer, if you have such a situation, is to focus on one bed or border that faces the sun, and work on breaking up the soil with lots of grit or gravel. Over time, your efforts should be rewarded with a soil of lighter composition that has a more hospitable pH level and provides better drainage. An inexpensive soil tester kit from the garden centre offers a precise enough reading for most gardeners. Many Mediterranean plants are lime lovers, and need a pH level that is neutral to alkaline in order to thrive.

Right: *The graceful flowers of* Tulipa sylvestris *and grape hyacinth grow amongst rosemary and lavender, as they would in the wild.*

RAIN AND FROST

Having high levels of rainfall should not in itself be a deterrent in growing drought-proof plants. In my own garden, we can have weeks of heavy winter rain and more again in early summer, followed by weeks of drought through high summer when my neighbour's lawn turns brown. The only plant to have suffered through heavy and continued summer rain is *Salvia argentea*, which has huge, felted leaves that are irresistible to slugs emerging after the rains. Placing a cloche or pane of glass over a plant prevents heavy winter rain from rotting vulnerable woolly-leaved plants such as *Lavandula lanata*. Otherwise, a gravel mulch works like a cosy, protective blanket on the

soil. My potted olive tree, with a mulch of big cobbles over the compost (soil mix), has survived outside through a few degrees of winter frost. I simply move it close to a sheltered wall to keep the worst of the weather off.

Contrary to popular belief, most Mediterranean native plants are frost hardy. If they are tough enough to withstand drought, they are tough enough to tolerate a few degrees of frost. So long as your garden does not have prolonged periods of severe frost, you can grow these plants successfully. My Mediterranean garden is actually in a frost pocket, but so far, because I have kept to the tough drought-resistant plants of *maquis* and *garrigue*, there have been no casualties except for a young prostrate rosemary, which was easily replaceable. Cloches and fleece can always be used as a safeguard in very cold weather, and warm walls offer protection at planting time to those plants that are more vulnerable, such as the pomegranate tree.

In fact, gardens in more temperate climates than the Mediterranean's have the edge, because they enjoy a long, milder summer: instead of Mediterranean plants burning out early in the year, the flowering show goes on and on and the colours grow ever richer. As the plants in neighbouring gardens teeter and fall, I smugly watch the pinks and yellows of the Mediterranean summer garden give way to the blues and purples of sea holly, hyssop, lavender and globe thistle, all the colours of a Mediterranean sky at its bluest.

Above: *In late summer, there is still plenty of colour and texture; wild leeks, blowing about in the wind like giant drumsticks, add a touch of drama.*

Right: *As summer gives way to autumn, the metallic blue flowerheads of* Eryngium *fade to ethereal silver and the bright blue bindweed continues to bloom.*

Above left: *Even after a heavy frost, or snow, the plants will emerge unscathed.*

Above right: *Frost lends the textural leaves of thyme a delicate, lacy beauty.*

Right: *Tough, resilient plants of the* maquis *are not only drought resistant, but frost resistant too.*

effective textures

Survival strategies

What makes Mediterranean plants able to tolerate long periods of drought? How can they thrive in such inhospitable conditions of stony, poor soil? There are various different ways in which these plants have adapted to their harsh native environment. Familiarizing yourself with their characteristics will give you confidence in their ability to thrive in your own garden.

LEAF REDUCTION
Plants that have plenty of moisture but limited light tend to have lush, broad leaves to maximize their light intake. In sharp contrast, many Mediterranean evergreens, such as lavender, thyme, rosemary and pine, have thin, needle-like leaves or lacy, dissected leaves that, by limiting their surface area, keep evaporation to a minimum and thus reduce water loss. Needle-like leaves such as those of rosemary are also arranged so that they shade each other from the full force of the sun.

TAP ROOTS
Some plants appear to thrive on shingle, sand or stone alone, but in fact they have long, questing roots that grow right down beneath the inhospitable surface to search for water. *Glaucium flavum*, *Tolpis barbata* and *Acanthus* are three examples.

SUCCULENTS
These plants have thick, fleshy leaves and stems – often roots, too – so they have plenty of storage space for water. Their hardened skins are designed to seal in moisture.

GREY LEAVES
Some Mediterranean plants have grey or near-white foliage that feels – and looks – as if it is made of wool or felt. Examples include *Lotus hirsutus*, *Phlomis* and *Salvia argentea*. If you look closely you will see that this tactile coat is actually composed of fine layers of hairs. These trap any moisture in the air, delivering it back to the plant, as well as limiting moisture loss from the plant and protecting it against the hot sun. The woolly or velvety coat also acts as a deterrent to browsing animals.

SILVER FOLIAGE
Plants such as *Convolvulus cneorum* have silvery foliage that seems to shimmer in the sun. In fact the leaves provide a reflective surface which deflects the sun's rays.

WAXY COATING
A waxy surface to the leaves helps reduce water loss by trapping it within an impermeable coat, and also acts as a sunshield. A good example is *Pittosporum tobira*.

Above: *The fine leaves and slender stems of lavender have a reduced surface area, so limit water loss.*

Above: *The thick, succulent leaves of this* Agave *store their own water supply to sustain the plant.*

Above: Lotus hirsutus *has woolly-textured foliage that is able to trap moisture from the air.*

Above: *The silver leaves of plants such as* Convolvulus cneorum *protect the plant by deflecting the sun's rays.*

Above: *The diverse kinds of foliage provide equally diverse ways of coping with drought.*

LOW, SCRUBBY HUMMOCKS

In exposed, windswept areas, often high up, plants literally crouch from the wind, becoming very scrubby and low-growing; they make themselves as small in volume as possible, minimizing their leaf size too, so that they are best able to resist whipping winds. *Armeria maritima*, growing on clifftops, is a prime example of this.

AROMATIC PLANTS

Plants with pungently scented leaves release their volatile oils in the heat to act as a physical sunscreen around the plant. The oils also inhibit water loss by transpiration.

BULBS, CORMS, TUBERS AND RHIZOMES

All these act as underground storehouses of energy, so when the season becomes too hot to handle, the plants simply shed their leaves and stems and retreat into the ground for a period of summer dormancy. Because they have food reserves, these plants are able to shoot up in early spring.

SUN LOVERS

Some Mediterranean flowers – and drought-tolerant plants in other comparable regions of the world – will only open when the sun appears. *Convolvulus sabatius*, for instance, stays tightly closed in the absence of sun, but soon opens its petals when the sun appears; *Anemone blanda*, *Lampranthus* and morning glory react in the same way. Other plants, notably rock roses and sun roses, open their flowers wide to greet the sun and, as dusk falls, their petals drop, leaving a carpet of colour on the ground beneath them.

Above: *The rock rose,* Cistus pulverulentus.

Left: Tulipa linifolia *retreats underground to save its strength so that it can burst into flower again the following spring.*

native plants

Mediterranean-type zones throughout the world

There are five areas in the world that have similar climates, and therefore ecosystems, to the Mediterranean region itself. The plants that grow in these arid areas have properties in both appearance and make-up similar to Mediterranean species, which enable them to tolerate hot, dry conditions. These five regions are southern and coastal central California, central Texas which includes Austin and San Antonio, central Chile, the South African Cape and south-western and southern Australia. Each region has its own equivalent to *maquis* and *garrigue*: fynbos in the Cape, chaparral in California and Texas, matorral in Chile, mallee scrub in Australia. Approximately 25,000 species of flowering plants occur wild in these five areas, and over half are found nowhere else. Together, they present quite a choice for the gardener.

If you live near these Mediterranean-type areas you might prefer to make a drought-proof garden using the local species, especially as they might be more readily available. Certainly the principles of planting outlined in this book will apply in exactly the same way. Thus, Californian chaparral plants, for instance, could include manzanita, Californian lilac, evening primrose, yucca, tree poppy, *Photinia*, blue lupin and *Fremontodendron*.

Above: *Californian poppy,* Eschscholzia californica, *is an exquisite annual, opening its petals wide as the sun warms them.*

Above: *English nurserywoman Beth Chatto illustrates in her gravel garden how plants from different zones can look sensational when creatively blended together.*

Above: *Rose campion,* Lychnis coronaria, *a native of south-eastern Europe, is a perfect candidate for the drought-proof garden and is easy and quick to grow.*

Above: *To a backdrop of tawny oat grass, hybrid achilleas that originate in eastern Europe harmonize with South African red hot pokers.*

Above: *The silver-ruffed heads of* Eryngium giganteum *make a striking contrast to the tall, wiry stems of purple* Verbena bonariensis, *a true prairie plant.*

Right: Lychnis coronaria *and euphorbia, classic* garrigue *plants, grow contentedly at the foot of golden-flowered* Genista aetnensis, *Mount Etna broom.*

GROWING NATIVE PLANTS

If you are fortunate enough to live in one of the five zones that have a similar climate to the Mediterranean and you wish to make a Mediterranean-style garden that is drought-resistant, easy to maintain and spectacularly colourful, then by all means use plants native to your region. So long as they behave in the same way as the Mediterranean plants described in this book then you will be successful. You could also be less of a purist and mix drought-proof plants from different regions, though you cannot for the most part leave the visual results to chance, as you can when you use native plants from one source. More artistry and intervention is needed to make them all look wonderful together, and care is needed so that one kind does not swamp another, and that the colours do not jar with each other.

The champion of this kind of gardening is the British plantswoman Beth Chatto. In the last few years she has created an exquisite gravel garden of drought-tolerant plants at her renowned show gardens in Colchester, Essex, an area which has one of the lowest rainfalls in Britain, averaging a scant 50cm/20in per year. Here you can find, growing cheek by jowl, Mediterranean cistus, South African diascia and Californian poppy, Mediterranean flax and South American vervain; thanks to Mrs Chatto's light touch, they look like a very magical form of *maquis*.

Left: Agapanthus, *the South African lily, produces its tall, elegant blooms in late summer and as well as white is available in many shades of blue.*

Below: *A symphony of mauves created with giant puffball heads of* Allium cristophii, Linum perenne, Verbena bonariensis *and* Tulbaghia violacea.

Left: *The stiff foliage fans of* Sisyrinchium striatum, *a native of South America, are reminiscent of the Mediterranean iris, and the flower spikes add to the vertical interest.*

Above: *Two callistemon shrubs from Australia, flanking an echium from the Canary Islands, reveal why they are commonly known as bottlebrushes.*

Above: *Two scrambling plants vie for space: Mediterranean blue bindweed* Convolvulus sabatius *and South American fleabane* Erigeron karvinskianus.

Above: *Satisfying foliage contrasts from drought-tolerant plants are provided by Asian bergenia, Mexican agave, the Korean ice plant* Sedum spectabile *and Mediterranean stachys.*

Grit, gravel and other groundwork

The conventional garden needs fertilizer and

manure to make plants prosper; the

stones

Mediterranean garden needs only stones to

make native plants feel perfectly at home.

pebbles

Here is how to give your garden drought-

proof status.

tough terrain

Getting soil into shape

Mediterranean plants grow in poor, stony soil in the wild, so that is exactly the environment you need to re-create in your Mediterranean garden. The French lavender that you admire in the herbaceous border originated on a Provençal hillside where the terrain is tough and rubbly. Not only does that lavender look completely at home in stony ground, but it feels at home, thriving in the sharp drainage that gritty, stony soil provides.

Mediterranean native plants hate getting their roots too wet: compacted, heavy soil holds water, so presents the worst hazard. While other gardeners' groundwork is all about enriching the soil, your groundwork is all about digging in gravel, shingle or grit to improve the texture. Don't be tempted to feed your Mediterranean plants or enrich the soil they are in, because the result will be weak, sappy growth. If your soil is excessively poor and dry, you might need to work in some organic matter to improve its ability to retain water.

Below: *Pale, creamy gravel complements the faded flowerheads of* Allium sphaerocephalon.

PREPARING THE SOIL
Although labour-intensive at the time, good soil preparation is essential and will ensure a trouble-free garden for years to come.

TOOLS AND MATERIALS
• spade
• 6–10mm/¼–½in gravel or pea shingle

1 △ When the soil is not wet or frozen, dig the whole area in a series of trenches, working backwards so that you do not compact the section you have worked. Throw gravel across each dug section of trench.

2 △ Turn the soil over from the next section on to the gravel, breaking up the earth as you go. Depending on the size of your trench, you may well have to use several spadefuls of gravel.

3 △ Work the gravel well into the soil. This will be hard work if your soil is clingy and clay-based.

4 △ When you have worked over the whole area, the soil should have a crumbly consistency and should not be sticky or form clods.

YOUR SOIL'S BEST ALLIES: STONE AND SHINGLE

Gravel is simply stone chippings that are cut from large rocks in a quarry. You can also use pea shingle, dredged from river beds: this is similar in size and shape but the edges have been eroded over time by water, so the stones are smoother and rounder. The advantage of using chippings is that, if your garden is plagued by slugs or snails, they will be more effectively deterred by the sharp, inhospitable edges of the stones. For mulch, choose a pale colour to provide contrast with the plants, but mix in occasional stones of varying shades – and larger sizes – to make the finished effect more natural.

HOW MUCH GRAVEL?

However much you think you need, you'll need lots more. You can never have too much gravel for a Mediterranean garden, as texturizer and mulch, to a depth of approximately 5cm/2in. A ton seems like a huge amount, but you will be surprised how quickly it goes.

WHAT SIZE STONES?

The right size gravel to mix into your soil is between 6mm/¼in and 10mm/½in, the size of a small, flattened pea; use the same gravel as a mulch. It is cheapest to buy in bulk from builders' suppliers, although garden centres and DIY stores stock gravel conveniently bagged. For smaller alpine-type plants and as a mulch for container plants, a coarse grit of about 4mm/⅙in is appropriate.

To complete your stock of stone, coarse stone chippings are useful for scattering over a mulch to create a natural effect, and for placing at the base of containers to improve drainage. Soft limestone chippings crush over time, but give the right setting for Mediterranean plants, which grow on limestone in their native habitat.

Above: *Where spaces of earth in a conventional garden look like black holes, in the Mediterranean garden, mulched with gravel, they become an integral part of the landscape.*

Above: *Keep a basic stock of stone chippings like these: limestone, top left, for scattering over mulch; gravel, top right, for soil texturizer and mulch; coarse grit, below, for smaller scale work.*

USING GRAVEL AS A MULCH

There are several good reasons to go for gravel as a mulch: it insulates plants; it holds in water for longer, reducing evaporation from the soil; it reflects sun back on to the plants; it makes a plant-flattering backdrop; it stops the crowns of plants from rotting in prolonged wet weather and keeps mud splashes off. As if that wasn't enough, gravel also makes the spaces between plants look good in a way that bare earth cannot, so that instead of conventional tight planting, with everything cheek by jowl, special plants can be grown in isolation to show them to advantage; grasses and light, airy plants, especially, look good set out in this way. The overall effect is more natural.

Right: Anemone blanda *settled in a cosseting blanket of gravel.*

low maintenance

Gravel or grass?

The traditional lawn is out of place in the Mediterranean garden: it is never happy without plenty of moisture and is a high-maintenance feature, whatever its size. And in these days of drought and water conservation, when the lawn is generally a crisp brown by late summer, gravel is becoming an increasingly attractive option.

If you decide to replace grass with gravel you will need to dig up the turf, lay down black landscape fabric and cover with 7.5cm/3in of consolidated coarse gravel. Then cover with a 5cm/2in layer of smaller size gravel, and compact with your feet, or a roller. The effect can be softened with pockets of planting. Another alternative is to carve an island bed in the centre of the grass, thus making more space for plants, less for lawn.

Above: *Small plants such as this* Veronica gentianoides *can be planted in gravel, blending borders and paths together.*

Above: *Gravel makes simple, low-maintenance paths that provide the perfect complement to Mediterranean plants.*

GRAVEL PATHS

Gravel is also the ideal medium for paths, either straight and formal or curvy and flowing.

In her superb gravel garden, Beth Chatto uses gravel to simulate dry river beds, flowing through drifts of plants. This makes for the most natural-looking kind of path, meandering interestingly in and around the plants, instead of stretching from A to B in a straight line. You can plant in this kind of free-flowing gravel path, and it will look as if the plant just landed there, on the wind. In fact, many do, spreading their seed into this receptive medium so that seedlings come up between the stones where they can be left to flourish, or easily prised out and replanted where you want. The stony soil, you will find, overwinters seedlings safely where heavier soil might rot them. As a bonus, unwanted plants – weeds – are usually easy to remove from gravel.

To make things simple, use the same gravel for paths as for planting. Then you can broaden the beds and narrow the paths, just by planting in the gravel. For a weed-free – and seedling-free – path, lay down black landscape fabric and use the same procedure as for replacing a lawn.

PLANTING THROUGH LANDSCAPE FABRIC

For areas of sparse planting, you might want to lay landscape fabric under the gravel to prevent weeds and seedlings appearing. Because this fabric – heavy-duty black woven polypropylene – keeps out light, plants do not grow through it. By cutting holes into it to make planting pockets, you have complete control over your Mediterranean landscape.

TOOLS AND MATERIALS
- landscape fabric (heavy-duty polypropylene)
- pegs
- large scissors or knife
- trowel
- plant
- gravel

1 △ Lay the landscape fabric over the prepared bed and peg down all round the edge. Make criss-cross slashes at each point where you want to position a plant.

2 △ Fold back the four points of the fabric to give you a square large enough to plant in. Dig out the earth until the planting hole is the correct size for the rootball.

3 △ Set the plant in the hole in the usual way and fill in with soil. Water in. Ease the black liner back a little, leaving enough space for water to reach the plant.

4 △ When the planting is complete, cover the whole area with gravel to a depth of about 5cm/2in. If you want to add more plants after the gravel is laid, simply push it aside before cutting through the fabric.

CONTROLLING WEEDS

Before beginning a Mediterranean terraced garden, cover each bed with black landscape fabric in order to eradicate all the weeds, but make pockets here and there for the plants you want to settle straight away. One season will kill off annual weeds, but persistent perennials will take a whole year or longer.

Above: *Cut black landscape fabric to fit and securely peg down on to the terraces from autumn through to the following spring.*

Above: *Patience pays off; once the weeds are eliminated, and the plants are settled in, quick progress will have been made in only one season.*

undulating layers

Terraces and raised beds

There can be no more typically Mediterranean landscape than a terraced hillside planted with grape vines or olive trees. The flat terraces make it easier to work the land, the stone walls create sheltered microclimates, and the tiered beds themselves offer wind protection and store heat, enabling growers to get an early start.

In a garden, exactly the same benefits apply. Low, easily traversed terraces can convert a straightforward sloping site into an intriguing design that makes gardening itself a real pleasure. Terraces also make wonderful "display shelves" for the plants, presenting them in layers that are best placed to receive the warmth of the sun. Trailing plants can tumble and fall from one bed over the wall on to the next, making a romantic, natural effect.

If you garden on any kind of a slope, give real consideration to making terraces before you do anything else. You will be delighted that you made the initial effort: ultimately, you will make your gardening effort-free, as well as adding another dimension to your garden.

In my garden, the terraces simulate the gentle contours of undulating, natural terracing with no straight lines. Low retaining walls have been constructed from reconstituted limestone bricks of different sizes, in sympathy with the limestone that Mediterranean plants grow in. Each is about 30cm/12in high, with "weep-holes" along the base just above ground level (made by leaving the mortar out of the vertical joints every so often). Each wall, of course, has a solid concrete foundation. Once the edge of each bed had been planted with prostrate rosemaries, thymes and helianthemums, it did not take long for them to tumble over the walls, so blurring the divisions between one terrace and another.

Left: *Terracing carved out of the hillside in Umbria, Italy, makes ideal conditions for growing olive trees, providing them with wind protection and a sheltered, warm microclimate.*

Right: *A garden on a slope in Tuscany is made far more interesting to look at – and to work in – by terracing it in local stone.*

Below: *Low, broad terraces make gardening a pleasure, and make display cases that show off the plants to advantage, as well as presenting them to the sun.*

Below right: *Planted in familiar stony terrain, plants soon settle and soften the edges of the low walls, so it becomes hard to tell where one terrace starts and the other finishes.*

RAISED BEDS

A raised bed follows the same principle as a terrace, the earth being held within a retaining wall of supporting stones or rocks. If your garden is completely flat, a few raised beds will add lots of character as well as making the landscape more suited to Mediterranean plants, whose natural habitat consists of rocky slopes and hillsides. A raised bed will also raise the temperature of the soil – which is why it is a good option for vegetable growing – making it all the cosier for Mediterranean habitués. Fill the bed with two parts garden soil or soil-based compost (soil mix) and one part grit, adding 10cm/4in of drainage material – broken crocks or pebbles – in the base first. Wait a week before planting to allow the soil to settle.

Another option to make your garden terrain more interesting is to raise the back part of a border to give a natural-looking terrace, so that your plants grow on different levels. This raised bed could be made merely from an informal retaining wall of well-placed rocks, at single height.

Top: *Pinks growing in a narrow trough provided by a dry stone wall have the perfect environment and showcase.*

Above: *A rustic stone terrace in an Italian country garden is made even more charming with the addition of pink and white* Erigeron karvinskianus *peppering the cracks.*

Above: *Raised beds of different heights not only add character to a garden, they raise the soil temperature and provide cosy conditions for Mediterranean plants.*

Right: *One way of coping with a steep slope is to landscape it with large stones, and plant in the nooks and crannies, as the owner of this seaside garden in Ireland has done.*

perfect environment

Making a stone trough

The smallest raised bed of all is the stone trough, which allows you to grow choice little Mediterranean plants in a perfect, closeted environment that also permits them to be admired close to. You could make a trough from limestone bricks quite cheaply – don't forget to allow a drainage hole at the base, covering it with a piece of wire grille – or mould one from concrete, which can look surprisingly rugged and stonelike.

This method involves digging a hole in the ground, and letting the concrete set around a mould of two plastic boxes. If possible, make the trough in late winter, when the ground is at its wettest, and leave it in the ground for three weeks to harden very slowly: this will render it frost-proof.

Right: Several varieties of houseleek quickly spread in a stone trough, making a rich tapestry.

TOOLS AND MATERIALS

- two plastic boxes, approximately 45 x 35 x 15cm/18 x 14 x 6in depth
- spade
- spirit level
- square 7cm/2¾in plastic flowerpot, top half cut away
- 9 spadefuls builder's sand
- 3 spadefuls coir compost
- 3 spadefuls cement
- wheelbarrow
- straight-sided piece of wood
- heavy-duty polythene (plastic) sheet
- scissors
- grit
- bubblewrap, if necessary
- sharp tool such as a screwdriver
- hammer
- wire brush

Left: Finished trough with Deschampsia *grass.*

1 △ *Select a piece of uncultivated ground in which to make your trough. Turn a plastic box upside down and mark out the size of the trough with a spade, roughly 5cm/2in larger than the box all round. Dig out a hole to the required depth of the finished trough.*

2 △ *Use a spirit level to check that the bottom of the hole is level and flat. Place the plastic pot in the centre of the hole, to form a drainage hole.*

3 △ *Mix the sand, coir compost and cement in a wheelbarrow. Add water and mix to a workable consistency; not too wet or too solid. Line the bottom of the hole with the resultant concrete to the level of the upturned pot and gently tamp it down with a piece of wood.*

4 △ *Take one plastic box and wrap it in a sheet of heavy-duty polythene (plastic). Fill the second box with grit and place it in the first plastic box to secure the polythene.*

5 △ *Centre the two boxes in the hole, then pour the concrete all around the edge to the required height (roughly the height of the plastic boxes). Tamp down the concrete all round. Cover the trough with polythene and leave to harden slowly for three weeks. If frost is expected, cover the trough with bubblewrap to protect it.*

6 △ *Dig out the ground around the trough, then lift out the plastic box mould. Lift the hardened trough out of the hole. Scrape the soil roughly off the sides and base using a spade. Remove the small pot and define the square hole it has left with a sharp tool.*

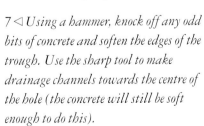

7 ◁ *Using a hammer, knock off any odd bits of concrete and soften the edges of the trough. Use the sharp tool to make drainage channels towards the centre of the hole (the concrete will still be soft enough to do this).*

8 ▷ *Brush with a wire brush to give it a weathered finish.*

smaller scale

Miniature Mediterranean gardens

Plants allowed to spread in troughs – miniature Mediterranean gardens, if you like – are inclined to do the most extraordinary things. When given its head the humble houseleek, for instance, grows upwards to form wonderful textural towers that merit close scrutiny. A few small plants of prostrate thyme or chamomile will spread to form a fragrant, tactile mat that it is impossible not to stroke. Dwarf species iris such as *Iris attica* look perfectly at home with the stony backdrop, as do piercingly blue gentians, which are used to growing among stones high in the Alps. Trailing plants such as the blue Mediterranean bindweed, *Convolvulus sabatius*, and the rock rose *Helianthemum nummularium* obligingly sprawl and tumble over the edge to form the prettiest of flowering cascades.

A stone trough is more suited to permanent residents, so gently dig them up and divide as they outgrow their space. Whatever your choice of plants – an assortment of plants and bulbs, or just one variety for maximum impact – use a soil-based compost (soil mix) such as John Innes No 2 mixed with the same amount of sharp grit to give

Left: *Five small thyme plants start to spread almost as soon as they are planted.*

Left: *Two months later, they have formed a green carpet and are starting to flower.*

Above: *Planted alongside tufa rock, electric blue gentians look as they do in the wild.*

Left: *Houseleeks surrounded by gravel make a marvellous effect of pattern on pattern.*

Above: *When they start growing upwards, houseleeks turn into the most exotic of plants.*

Left: *The trailer* Convolvulus sabatius *is ideally suited to the restrictions of the trough.*

Left: *Three months on, the bindweed is producing a profusion of tumbling blue flowers.*

the best possible drainage. Make a shallow layer of small stones at the base, then fill with compost mix and insert the plants. To give you an idea of planting space, in a trough measuring 30 x 36cm/12 x 14in five creeping thymes will give quick coverage, but just one plant will eventually cover the surface completely. Six *Iris attica*, evenly spaced, are plenty, and just three *Convolvulus sabatius* will quickly spread. Plant houseleeks (*Sempervivum*) according to your patience; three will quickly multiply. Add a little fertilizer when planting to compensate for the restricted growing conditions, but don't overfeed the plants, because you don't want them to outgrow their space. Cover the compost with a blanket of grit, making sure that crowns and rosettes are protected with plenty of grit around their bases. Finally, site your Mediterranean mini garden raised on bricks by a seat in the sun, for everyone to enjoy.

mosiac patterns

Making a patio simpatico

Mediterranean courtyards are created from cobblestones, not concrete, so before you start planting your containers, convert the area on which they stand to something a little more exciting if you are faced with an unforgiving or uneven floor surface. A cobblestone mosaic would be ideal, but it is simpler to throw down a thick carpet of gravel: this will even up the surface and cover a multitude of imperfections. Not only will it create instant Mediterranean status, but it will give your pots valuable drainage. Make it at least 5cm/2in thick to be effective, and choose a pale, plant-flattering shade or a blend of similar-coloured stones.

Now for the fun. On this neutral base, add a glamour element: sparkling mosaic-like patterns that are in fact random scatterings of coloured pebbles, inexpensive gemstones or mosaic chips in glass, stone or plastic; a movable, floating floor that you can make as simple or as elaborate as you choose. And from day to day, the pattern and form will vary. Stone steps can be enlivened, too, with a line of coloured stones across the tread.

Be sure to choose a medium that will not shatter when you walk on it; slate and shells, for example, would not be suitable, unless as a border frieze where they would not be disturbed. Small terracotta or decorative glazed tiles set at intervals into the gravel can make an effective stepping-stone path in and around containers.

Above: *Play up the colours of flowers – and painted pots – with harmonizing and contrasting gemstones that sparkle in the sun.*

Left: *Transform a dull concrete patio by shovelling gravel on to the bare surface.*

Left: *Distribute the gravel evenly with a rake.*

Above: *The mellow terracotta tones of the pots are echoed by Moroccan-style tiles of the same material.*

Below: *Small pieces of tile add segments of colour and interest to a plain gravel surface.*

Above: *Pieces of coloured tile add an unusual charm to stone steps.*

Making maquis

Forget the colour wheel, planting plans, and

worrying about how to have a succession of

natural planting

flowers through the year; instead, learn from

nature, and have a garden full of plant

natural growth

partners that were made for each other.

Using landscapes

Plan nothing at all when you plant, and your Mediterranean garden will look wonderful, because all the plants grow naturally together in the Mediterranean landscape, and make good companions for one another. Nature always gets it right. Nothing will jar, and you will delight in the many novel effects and dazzling colour combinations – hot pink and tangerine, saffron and powder blue, sharp lemon and piercing violet – that occur all by themselves. But there are ways of pushing Nature just a little to achieve even more spectacular results.

TRAILING PLANTS
Encourage trailing plants to cascade over low walls so that they conceal the brick or stone, and tumble on to the plants beneath, creating a natural effect. These can include prostrate rosemaries, trailing – not upright – creeping thymes, *Convolvulus sabatius*, *Helianthemum* and *Euphorbia myrsinites*.

Left: *Plant rock roses along the edge of a low stone wall to make cascades of colour.*

Below: *Just one plant of prostrate rosemary soon spreads to blur boundaries between terraces.*

GRAVEL PATHWAYS
Leave gravel trails through plants for pathways so you can wander amongst them, savouring their fragrances. You will also find that some plants, especially tall, airy plants and grasses, look better for having space around them.

Above: *Creeping lemon thyme* Thymus serpyllum *'Lemon Curd' forms evergreen mats that soften hard landscape.*

Right: Allium sphaerocephalon *and orange poppies spread out amongst the gravel.*

INSTANT ANNUALS

Do not worry if your Mediterranean garden or border starts out as a sea of stone or gravel; it is not like a herbaceous border that you need to fill instantly. It can be added to gradually, and will look fine at each stage. You can also sow annuals to make instant but temporary colour shots.

GROWING THROUGH STONES

Push different sized stones around the base of small plants to suggest that they have grown up between the stones, and leave spaces in hard landscaping for planting pockets. After a season or two, you will find that plants – *Lavandula stoechas*, thyme, hellebores and so on – will have self-seeded in stony nooks and crannies naturally.

Above: *Cistus, planted in the cracks between stones, looks as if it had sprung up there naturally.*

Above: *To add a touch of bright colour, the annual lupin* Lupinus varius *grows by a young Judas tree.*

Left: *The annual poppy* Papaver carmeli *makes a bigger splash amongst a landscape of pale stone.*

ADDING VERTICALS

Use verticals to contrast with mound-forming shrubs, and emulate the look of slimline cypresses in the Mediterranean landscape. Two good small-scale verticals are the upright box *Buxus sempervirens* 'Greenpeace', and narrow conifer *Juniperus communis* 'Sentinel'.

Above: *In this Mediterranean garden, cypress trees add vertical interest to the planting at Tresco in the Scilly Isles.*

Textural tricks

FAMILIAR FAVOURITES

Don't rip out plants in your old garden or border because you think they do not qualify; many widely grown garden plants originate in the Mediterranean, such as lavender, helianthemum, euphorbia, *Viburnum tinus*. If you have any herbs – rue, rosemary, helichrysum, santolina – the chances are they are Mediterranean, too. Look first, and either dig plants up and move them, plant around them, or take cuttings.

Left: *Two popular garden herbs,* Helichrysum italicum *and artemisia, have their roots firmly in the Mediterranean.*

ARCHITECTURAL PLANTS

Plant stand-out architecturals amongst the shrubby hummocky shapes, such as acanthus and *Salvia sclarea* var. *turkestanica.* Don't worry that these last two don't perform in winter: bare gravel, unlike bare earth, is not ugly.

Right: Salvia sclarea *var.* turkestanica *forms a majestic shape that provides contrast to lower growing, rounded shrubs.*

Left: *All these Mediterranean native plants are also stalwarts of many gardens: euphorbia, purple sage, lavender, iris.*

DECORATIVE FOLIAGE

Use the matt, felty leaves of *Stachys byzantina* to lap around the base of French lavenders; the invaluable smoky purple leaves of *Salvia officinalis* Purpurascens Group to conceal the leggy stems of ice green *Phlomis italica*, and flatter the pink flowers; the woolly apple green stems of *Ballota pseudodictamnus* and grey ones of *Lotus hirsutus* to make textural statements wherever you fancy.

Above: *The soft muted tones of purple sage act as a neutral colour connector between the more vibrant stachys, euphorbia and lavender flowers.*

Above: *The complex leaf formation of* Ballota pseudodictamnus *complements the flowers of rock rose and* Halimium lasianthum.

DRAMATIC CONTRASTS

To create the maximum impact, team together plants that not only have contrasting colours, but also have shape and texture that are dramatically different. Try dark, feathery bronze fennel alongside the flat, broad leaves of silvery *Salvia argentea*; prickly, green-stemmed *Genista lydia* next to smooth grey-leaved rock roses.

Right: *Rounded heads of* Allium sphaerocephalon *make a sparky combination with cistus flowers and jagged* Eryngium *flowers.*

Left: *The starry heads of metallic blue eryngium contrast with the lemon bobble flowers of santolina.*

ALTERNATING TEXTURES

Play down colour by making harmonious partners from same-shade plants, but play up their diverse textures. Consider shiny silver *Convolvulus cneorum* with the pale felty leaves of *Stachys byzantina*; the tufted flowerheads of French lavender with the more familiar flowers of English lavender.

Right: *Create a pool of moody blue with textural contrasts, courtesy of sea holly* Eryngium *and globe thistle* Echinops.

take a leaf from nature

Weaving colour

HOT COLOUR

For pockets of singing colour through the garden, use *Calendula officinalis*. The sharp orange flowerheads sizzle with shocking pink cistus. Viper's bugloss *Echium vulgare* has fuzzy blue flower spikes that look stunning alongside the pot marigolds; a biennial, count on it flowering every other year. For instant planting, buy plants that will flower for the coming season.

Right: *Marigolds growing up amongst the blue flower spikes of viper's bugloss provide a sizzling contrast.*

TRAILING BINDWEED

Learn to love bindweed. It won't be hard, considering one Mediterranean variety has powder blue flowers, the other, silver stems and shell pink flowers: *Convolvulus sabatius* and *C. althaeoides*, respectively. Use them liberally to trail through other plants which would be enhanced by borrowing the flowers.

Below: Convolvulus althaeoides *twines around the silver stems of lemon-flowered* Helichrysum italicum.

Above: *Pink bindweed* Convolvulus althaeoides *winds through the dusky leaves of purple sage.*

Above:*The glaucous rosettes of* Euphorbia myrsinites *are perfect partners for blue* Convolvulus sabatius.

Above: Salvia officinalis 'Icterina' *makes a fresh variegated foliage backdrop for the blue flowers of* Convolvulus sabatius.

SIZZLING CONTRASTS

Raise the colour impact by placing flowering plants together that offer the greatest possible contrast to one another: cerise with lemon, purple with sharp orange, deep blue with yellow.

Above: *The shock value of pink next to yellow coronilla is strengthened by the golden centres of the cistus flowers.*

Above: *The dark-centred yellow flowers of* Tolpis barbata *are the perfect complement to the rich blue flowers of* Anagallis monellii.

COMPLEMENTARY FOLIAGE

Use foliage plants to highlight neighbouring flowering plants by choosing them to provide maximum contrast not just in colour but in shape and texture too. Choose evergreen varieties to provide year-round interest.

Above: *The woolly, palest grey flowers and foliage of* Stachys byzantina *flatter the flowers of the gallica rose.*

resilient plants

Planting the Mediterranean garden

Planting in the traditional garden often involves arduous digging in of manure and fertilizers, followed by diligent watering until the plants are established. In the Mediterranean garden, by contrast, so long as you have begun by mixing plenty of gravel with the soil, very little further work is needed, and wherever your spade strikes, it will sink into well-drained soil.

Planting is a pleasure because it is so easy and so quick. Because Mediterranean natives are habitués of poor soils, they do not need pampering with feeds and fertilizers. Manure is anathema to them and will simply make their growth sappy. Herbs are at their most aromatic and flavourful not only sited in sunny locations, but growing in undernourished soil.

PLANTING MADE EASY

All you need to do to make a Mediterranean plant feel at home is the following: the procedure doesn't vary.

TOOLS AND
MATERIALS
• trowel or spade
• grit or gravel
• plant
• watering can

Left: *Stony soil provides the conditions that stachys and ballota thrive on.*

1 △ *Make a planting hole, using a trowel or spade. The hole should be substantially larger than the rootball, so that the plant is not cramped.*

2 △ *Throw a handful of grit or gravel into the hole. Knock the plant out of its pot. If it has substantial roots, tease them out so that they grow into the ground.*

3 △ *Ease the plant into place so that the top of the rootball is level with the surface of the soil.*

4 △ *Work the soil in around the plant, and firm in with clenched fists. Water well and add a 5cm/2in mulch of gravel around the plant base.*

WHY MULCH?

Any kind of mulch – a thick coverlet over the soil – helps to keep moisture in the ground. Traditional herbaceous perennials benefit from a layer of well-rotted manure, and a seemingly inhospitable blanket of stones benefits Mediterranean plants, in several ways:

• A gravel mulch conserves moisture.

• It insulates plants in winter, and protects the crowns and rosettes of felty-foliaged plants from rotting.

• It absorbs heat, and the pale colour of the stones reflects the sun's rays to the plant.

• It makes an attractive backdrop, showing flowers and foliage to advantage.

PLANTING DISTANCES

A gravel mulch makes the gaps between newly planted additions look not only acceptable, but positively attractive, unlike the gloomy blankness of bare earth. Where the temptation in the conventional border is to plant too close in order to have as little bare soil as possible on display, the Mediterranean garden can be

Above: *After planting, add a blanket of coarse gravel across the area to connect the collar of gravel around each plant and make the spaces visually appealing.*

Right: *Plants settled into their new home will soon spread and eventually will leave little gravel on display.*

Above: *Before they spread to form one clump, these pinks look good growing in splendid isolation.*

sparsely planted to start with; indeed it should be because, given the optimum conditions, the plants will soon spread and sprawl.

Shrubs can be planted singly, but to create a mat of thyme or sage, say, plant three small herb plants 23cm/9in apart, and they will quickly merge to make one substantial specimen. In the first year, if you want to fill a few gaps, interplant with annuals such as borage and pot marigold.

WHEN TO PLANT

Autumn is traditionally the time for garden planting, but container plants can be planted at any time so long as the ground is workable. If you are planting a whole Mediterranean garden, or even a border, it is best to do so in spring, so that the young plants do not have to start life fighting a potentially cold, damp winter, but can get their roots down comfortably and, in many cases, still have time to build up flowers for the coming summer.

tapestry lawn

Making an island bed

An island bed is one big glorious excuse to grow the prettiest plants that can be admired at close quarters, or present an impressionist effect from far off. It is also a way of losing some of the lawn without digging up the whole thing, as well as turning over an area of humdrum high maintenance to low-maintenance glamour. The beauty of the island bed – you could call it a tapestry lawn – is its flexibility. The one shown in the making is simply carved from the centre of the lawn in a vague amorphous circle, with a sundial positioned in the middle to give it some focus. At its widest point it is 2.7m/9ft, but it can easily be made larger at any time. Having no formal boundary makes this easy, but you could edge the bed with a ring of upright thyme, teucrium or dwarf box.

TOOLS AND MATERIALS
• wine bottle
• sand
• spade
• 4mm/⅙in grit (about 300kg/6cwt for a circular bed 2.7m/9ft diameter)
• low-growing mat plants, alpines, herbs, grasses and bulbs (about 80 plants)
• trowel
• watering can

1 △ Mark out the shape of the bed by pouring sand from a wine bottle.

2 △ Skim off the turf and dig over the soil. Add grit and work in thoroughly, breaking up any clods of earth.

3 △ Keeping plants in their pots, arrange them on the bed, moving them around until you are happy with their positions.

4 △ Plant and water in thoroughly. Make a collar of grit around each plant to finish.

5 △ Add a 5cm/2in layer of grit to cover the whole bed, and add different-sized stones here and there to give it an authentic feel.

Above: *The completed island bed, in flower a scant six weeks after planting.*

Above: *In full flower, viper's bugloss* Echium vulgare *makes a fittingly dramatic plant to accompany the silvery, wirewool foliage of* Artemisia alba 'Canescens'.

Above: *A few months after planting,* Stipa tenuifolia *produces a thick silken fringe of shimmering silky blonde that sways sensuously in the summer breeze.*

Plants for an island bed

Not all these plants are Mediterranean natives, but most of them are, and the rest blend beautifully; the trick is to go for alpines, dwarf varieties and low-lying mat formers such as rock roses, geraniums and thrift, scrubby herbs such as thyme and French tufted lavender *Lavandula stoechas*, and some grasses for height and movement. All of these should suit an open, sunny site with sharply drained soil. The plants are used in groups of three, each plant set a little apart; this is not just to give instant bulk but because the three plants will eventually merge into one. In the meantime, thanks to the blanket of grit, the spaces in between the plants do not matter at all.

To give an indication of how quickly these plants make themselves at home, the bed was planted in mid-spring, and the final photographs taken just six weeks later. In early summer, pretty pastel shades predominate, but later in the season the picture grows richer and moodier. Viper's bugloss throw up their rich blue spires, the grasses form tall, feathery plumes, the sea holly produces steely blue flowerheads and the deep plum houseleeks make strange chunky towers topped with flowers. And when you think the show has died down, up shoot the stems of *Allium sphaerocephalon*, topped with claret-coloured flowers, here and there among the gravel.

Allium insubricum: allium with pink nodding heads

Allium karataviense: large pink flowers on short stems, broad strappy foliage

Alyssum spinosum var. *roseum*: silvery foliage, tiny pink flowers

Armeria maritima 'Corsica': brick-flowered thrift

Artemisia alba 'Canescens': silver wiry foliage

Centaurea bella: pink cornflowers, silver foliage

Cytisus x *beanii*: dwarf yellow-flowered broom

Dianthus 'Little Jock': highly scented pink

Echium vulgare: viper's bugloss

Erodium 'Fran's Delight': mauve flowers, silver foliage

Eryngium variifolium: sea holly: serrated leaves, thistle flowers

Festuca glauca: stumpy grey grass

Geranium cinereum var. *subcaulescens*: magenta geranium

Geranium sanguineum var. *striatum*: dainty geranium with veined, soft pink flowers

Geranium tuberosum: bulbous lilac-flowered geranium

Helianthemum 'Cheviot': apricot rock rose, grey foliage

Helianthemum 'Fire Dragon': flame rock rose, larger than most, with grey foliage

Helianthemum 'Rhodanthe Carneum': pastel pink rock rose, grey foliage

Helianthemum 'Wisley Primrose': lemon rock rose, grey foliage

Lavandula angustifolia 'Nana Alba': dwarf white lavender

Lavandula stoechas: French lavender, with tufted mauve flowers

Origanum rotundifolium: decorative oregano, lime green bracts

Ornithogalum nutans: green-streaked white spiky flowers

Salvia officinalis 'Purpurascens': purple-leaved sage

Saponaria 'Bressingham': deep pink soapwort, foliage cushion

Sempervivum 'Rosie': dark red houseleek

Stipa tenuifolia: tall swishy grass

Teucrium x *lucidrys*: evergreen subshrub with tight foliage, pink flowers

Thymus pseudolanuginosus: woolly thyme

Thymus serpyllum 'Goldstream': creeping thyme with gold and green leaves

Verbascum phoeniceum 'Flush of White': white flowers

Veronica austriaca Corfu form: lavender flower spires

Above: *The pretty brick flowers of* Armeria maritima *'Corsica' are held above tussocks of foliage.*

Above: *Upright* Stipa *grass contrasts with* Geranium cinereum *var.* subcaulescens *and wiry* Alyssum spinosum.

Above: *Next to* Geranium sanguineum *var.* striatum, *dwarf broom* Cytisus × beanii *produces rich yellow flowers.*

Above: *The dusky coloured houseleeks are planted as rosettes, but soon start to tower upwards.*

Above: *White verbascums, apricot rock roses and lavender-coloured* Veronica *spires make a quiet corner.*

Above: *Textural mats of flower and foliage from rock roses, thyme, oregano and thrift.*

Plants for the shade

Even the Mediterranean garden has areas of shade that need specialized planting. These might be under a deciduous tree, or beneath the canopy of an evergreen, where shade is denser; they might be created by the shadows of walls, or lightly shaded areas beneath an overhead walkway or in a courtyard. Here are some suggestions for plants to suit these slightly trickier sites; the colours they afford will be less vibrant than those of flowers luxuriating in the sunlight, but they present a convincing case for a cool corner.

Above: *Shade-loving ferns in containers are content in this tiled, Portuguese garden.*

ACANTHUS ***

This imposing perennial has architectural foliage that inspired the scroll-like leaves carved on the columns of ancient Greece. *Acanthus mollis* has broad, rounded leaves but *Acanthus spinosus*, living up to its

Acanthus mollis.

Greek name *akanthos*, "thorn", has spiny, serrated leaves with prickly tips. Both species produce a large spike of hooded flowers, coloured ice pink and dusky burgundy, in late summer. Acanthus works well in groups of three – in a Portuguese botanical garden it grows as an entire enchanted forest, widely planted beneath trees. Give the basal leaves space to spread. It is simple to divide clumps when they become overcrowded after flowering. The only drawback with *Acanthus* is that it dies down in winter.

BUXUS SEMPERVIRENS ***

Forget for a moment the image of clipped topiary, and consider box as it grows in Mediterranean wildland: freeform, flowering, fruiting, even –

and with its own quiet, glossy-leaved appeal. Useful as a dense evergreen in light and shade, it can also be used as a screen or hedge. The cultivar 'Greenpeace' has an upright growth, making a slender column that contrasts with rounded shrubs.

Buxus sempervirens.

Geranium phaeum.

Helleborus foetidus.

Vinca minor 'Aureovariegata'.

GERANIUM PHAEUM ***

One of the most beautiful of the cranesbill geraniums is also one of the most accommodating. The aptly named mourning widow geranium has small, dainty flowers of the deepest, darkest claret or moody purple that appear from late spring; in some forms these can be white, which helps lighten dark corners, or variants between the two. Usefully, the leaves remain in winter.

HEDERA HELIX
'Oro di Bogliasco' ***

This name sounds wonderfully rococo but in fact describes one of the most common garden ivies, 'Goldheart', which has sunny yellow splashes on its rich green leaves. The former Italian name has now replaced 'Goldheart' internationally. Whatever its name, this ivy is indispensable as wall or ground cover, to brighten shady, dry places. Start off small, because its aerial pads will grip as it grows, and it grows quickly.

HELLEBORUS ***

An invaluable perennial for flowering in winter, the unjustly named stinking hellebore, *Helleborus foetidus*, is a native of scrub and woodlands in Europe as well as parts of the Mediterranean. It forms clumps of dark green, fan-like evergreen leaves and long-lasting clusters of pale green bellflowers, edged with dark red. Divide overcrowded clumps in spring. *Helleborus argutifolius* is a robust native of Corsica and Sardinia. It produces stiff stems of saw-edged leaves and pale green cupped flowers from late winter to early summer.

PULMONARIA SACCHARATA ***

The bristly-haired perennial Bethlehem sage produces white spotted leaves and, in spring, the prettiest borage-type flowers – they come from the same family – of blue and pink. Some types produce white flowers. It is a woodland plant that thrives in shade.

VINCA ***

Not the most exciting of plants, but the fresh evergreen leaves and violet or white flowers have a simple charm, and what the periwinkle lacks in thrills, it makes up for in usefulness. It is indispensable as ground cover where little else will grow, and at its best falling in cascades over low walls. *Vinca major* spreads like wildfire by rooting its stems, so consider the slightly less invasive *Vinca minor*.

Hedera helix *'Oro di Bogliasco'*.

Pulmonaria saccharata.

EVERGREENS FOR SHADE
Phillyrea angustifolia or
P. latifolia
Prunus lusitanica
Bupleurum fruticosum

BULBS FOR SEMI-SHADE
Cyclamen
Ornithogalum nutans
Lilium martagon
Hermodactylus tuberosus
Iris foetidissima

dappled arbours

Refuge from the sun

Pergolas and arbours provide cool, shady respite from the heat of the day. Perhaps there is less burning need to create a refuge from the sun in your garden if you live in a more temperate climate, but such a structure, simple to build, presents another perspective, as well as an opportunity to grow a whole range of vines and climbers. Eating under the dappled shade of a vine-laden pergola is surely one of the great pleasures of the Mediterranean garden.

In Tuscany, the locals make pergolas from wooden poles crafted from mountain oak or pine for a simple shelter that is eminently rustic yet has its own charm. Grand gilded structures would not be in sympathy with the surroundings. However, bear in mind that smooth, machine-rounded poles will last longer than those with bark left intact, and softwood will need to have been pressure-treated with a preservative. Metal "shoes" set into the ground to hold posts are vital to stop even hardwood from eventually rotting.

Nowadays, easy-to-assemble kits for pergolas, arbours and arches are available in both rustic style, with larch poles or similar, and traditional, with timber posts which should be at least 10cm/4in thick for verticals and crossbeams. To make yours climber-friendly, secure plastic-covered wire to each post with vine eyes.

Above: *A long, shady walkway, flanked by lavender, is simply made from rustic poles attached to the side of the house.*

Left: *Living shade in the form of a thick conifer canopy provides cool and effective respite from the sun.*

Above: *Exotic blooms, given freedom to tumble from the pergola, and artfully arranged earthenware pots make this shady corner a magical one.*

Above: *In a shady courtyard in southern Italy, climbing roses clad a simple framework above the dining table.*

Right: *This terrace has dappled shade afforded by nothing more sophisticated than an overhead tramline of wires along which the vines can scramble.*

enticing ramblers

Climbers and vines

Pergolas, arbours and other frames have another function apart from providing shade: they present heaven-sent opportunities to be swagged and garlanded with leafy vines, trumpet-flowered climbers and rampaging roses.

Climbers have a more fundamental role to play, too. You are probably not blessed with a row of cypress trees as an ideal garden boundary or perhaps do not have stone walls. In other words, if you have a garden fence that rather ruins the effect of your carefully planted *maquis* beneath it, climbers, planted cleverly, will cover and conceal. Giving the fence a fronting of trellis on battens will ensure that they get a firm hold. You could paint both fence and trellis a soft blue, emulating an Aegean blue sky, so that beguiling glimpses peek through the foliage and flowers. If part of your garden boundary is an unforgiving concrete wall, wash it a pretty shade of rose pink, cover it with vine eyes and wires, and send purple morning glory swarming over it.

Above: *Common passion flower* Passiflora caerulea *is one of the most glamorous climbers; it is an American native but is widely grown in the Mediterranean.*

Left: *The scarlet passion flower* Passiflora coccinea *is grown outdoors in the mildest parts of the Mediterranean, but elsewhere it should be grown under glass.*

Right: *Despite its favoured habitat of scrub or hedgerow, morning glory* Ipomoea purpurea *should be valued as an exotic climber for the garden.*

Above: *The original sweet pea of Sicily has the sweetest scent of all, and it is easy to grow from seed.*

Left: *Roses, such as this yellow noisette climbing rose 'Claire Jacquier', are popular in Mediterranean gardens but need careful maintenance.*

Climbers will give your Mediterranean garden depth and drama. Try any of these: Tuscan honeysuckle, scented evergreen jasmine, ornamental vines, decorative trailing gourds, the wild sweet peas of the region and, for winter flowers, evergreen Balearic clematis. In Mediterranean gardens, roses are popular too, frequently dripping from wooden pergolas. If you want to include them in your Mediterranean garden, bear in mind that they will need watering, and appreciate richer soil than Mediterranean plants. Choose colours and forms that mesh with *maquis* plants; the scented rambler 'Veilchenblau' has dusty mauve flower clusters, at their best in partial shade, and 'Casino' is a climber with scented yellow flowers that make an ideal backdrop to the rich, opulent colours of the Mediterranean garden.

Climbers in the Mediterranean wild, as well as in gardens, are not well-behaved; they tend to trail, tumble and cascade around other plants as well as up and over walls. Shrubby Italian honeysuckle *Lonicera implexa* will twirl beguilingly around a small evergreen conifer or upright box, when planted alongside; encourage the union by curving a stem around the conifer and securing on the ground with a stone. Coax late-flowering *Clematis viticella* to tangle with a vine – *Vitis vinifera* 'Purpurea' makes a suitably sultry companion – and let honeysuckle *Lonicera etrusca* have its scented, flowering head. When evergreens, or evergreys, have flowered, weave wild violet or cerise sweet peas through and around them, like fairy lights through a tree. You can engineer this precisely by planting three or four young plants around a shrub, and encouraging them as they grow to tangle artlessly around the stems. Santolinas and helichrysums are perfect candidates for the sweet pea treatment, especially when they are producing their lemon or yellow flowerheads. The sweet pea flowers that bob above them look like dancing, darting butterflies.

Mediterranean climbers

Use the following climbers to add an exciting dimension to your Mediterranean garden. Throw away any stakes that accompany plants you buy at the nursery, but keep a supply of sweet pea rings and twist ties in your pockets to gently coerce them in the right direction as they twist through other plants and ramble over walls.

BOUGAINVILLEA FT
The bad news about bougainvillea is that you must offer it a frost-free, sheltered, warm site; the good news is apparent. Gardeners in cooler climates must grow it in a container, and dream.

CAMPSIS RADICANS **
The vigorous trumpet vine is an American native, but is grown so widely in Mediterranean gardens and parks that it merits inclusion here. Besides, those tubular flame flowers will look so spectacular in your garden that you won't mind where it comes from. It is a deciduous shrub that climbs with aerial roots like ivy, but tie it in initially. Keep it under tight control: it can reach 10m/33ft.

CLEMATIS CIRRHOSA **
Give this frequenter of woods and scrub a warm, sheltered wall, and it will perform wonders, covering it quickly with wiry red stems and the daintiest divided evergreen leaves, and from winter through spring producing creamy bellflowers speckled with plum and scented with honey. Ancient Greeks used it for making garlands. The variety *balearica*, from the Balearic Isles, has paler flowers with more pronounced freckles. Reaches 3m/10ft.

CLEMATIS VITICELLA ***
Usefully flowering in late summer, this clematis has abundant, small purple flowers that look spectacular en masse. The variety 'Etoile Violette' has richer violet flowers. Cut the stems back to the lowest pair of buds before growth starts in early spring. Reaches 4m/13ft.

Bougainvillea.

Campsis radicans.

Clematis cirrhosa *var.* balearica.

Clematis *'Etoile Violette'*.

Lathyrus tingitanus.

Vitis vinifera *'Purpurea'*.

IPOMOEA PURPUREA *FT*

The common morning glory might grow on scrubland in the Mediterranean, but it still makes a gorgeous garden plant to twine up walls or around railings. An easy-to-sow and grow annual, its large, intense purple, sometimes pink, flowers are all the more beautiful for their fleeting appearance with the sun. Can reach 3m/10ft.

LATHYRUS

Lathyrus odoratus *** is the original sweet pea and, some would say, unbeatable. First described as growing in Sicily, it has an intense scent and deep carmine and violet flowers. Sow this annual in spring, in deep pots, but for the chunkiest plants, sow the previous autumn. *Lathyrus tingitanus* **, the Tangier sweet pea, has exquisite deep rose flowers and grows so fast it is best sown in spring.

LONICERA **

The hedgerow honeysuckle of the Mediterranean region, the Etruscan honeysuckle – *Lonicera etrusca* – has richly fragrant yellow, white and pink flowers and blue-tinged, deciduous foliage. The red berries are a bonus. Best in full sun, the scrambling stems can reach 4m/13ft. Leathery-leaved *Lonicera implexa* is similar but shrubbier, smaller and an evergreen.

TRACHELOSPERMUM JASMINOIDES **

Another imposter, but from the East, the widely grown evergreen star jasmine has glossy green pointed leaves and sweet-scented, jasmine-like flowers. Give it a sheltered, warm wall or keep it clipped in a container as a luscious, exotic-looking shrub. Can reach over 8m/26ft.

VITIS VINIFERA ***

A grapevine is practically compulsory in the Mediterranean garden. For leafy cover, try the variety 'Brant' which is the vine best suited to hardy situations, yet produces dessert grapes. In autumn, the leaves turn shades of scarlet, russet, gold and pink. *Vitis vinifera* 'Purpurea' is an ideal backdrop to grey and silver shrubs, because the foliage is a dusky prune colour, turning a shade deeper in autumn. The small bunches of grapes hang like porcelain drop earrings.

Lonicera etrusca.

Trachelospermum jasminoides.

sublime perfume

Lavender: the flower of Provence

It is small wonder that when the Romans brought lavender to the Mediterranean, it took to the sunny slopes of the Alps, settled there, and spread. Now, unsurprisingly, lavender is one of the best-loved flowering plants, growing in gardens throughout the world, growing wild in the Mediterranean, Canary Isles and India, and growing in the fields around Grasse, in Provence.

At the start of the 20th century, France's government and perfume houses agreed to finance the planting of lavender fields for cultivation. Now Grasse is the world's largest lavender producer, but it is testament to lavender's easy-going nature that this sublimely scented flower is produced for perfume in countries worldwide, including Great Britain, Russia and the United States.

Above: *A huge bush of wild tufted lavender grows on a mountain slope in Morocco.*

WHICH LAVENDERS TO PLANT?

In your own Mediterranean garden, where you can cultivate lavender for its flowers and evergreen foliage as well as its perfume, make your first choice *Lavandula stoechas*, French lavender. The fir green foliage and blue mauve flowers, tufted like rabbits' ears, are a familiar sight in the pine forests, roadsides, open *maquis* and *garrigue* of the Mediterranean. It is a compact, stocky plant that is said to be doubtfully hardy, but it will happily survive several degrees of frost.

Its close relative *L. stoechas* ssp. *pedunculata* is even more flamboyant; the flowers have a pinker tone, with longer trailing tufts redolent of butterflies. I have found it to be as tough as *L. stoechas*. The fine-leaved foliage, as aromatic as the flowers, is a pale apple green. Both *stoechas* lavenders have a clean, camphorous note to the familiar

Lavandula stoechas.

Lavender st. *ssp* pedunculata.

Lavandula pinnata.

lavender fragrance, and are the first lavenders to flower in the garden, in late spring. *L. lanata*, of mountains and screes, is another gem, with leaves that look as if they have been cut from white felt. *L. angustifolia*, as well as *L. latifolia*, is the common wild lavender of the Mediterranean, with the more familiar rich mauve flower spikes and almost grey leaves. From *L. angustifolia*, and from *L. × intermedia*, a cross between the two, many garden cultivars have been produced, so that there is a wide choice from white through pink to rich purple, all, like the type, totally hardy. For the finest fragrance, though all lavenders smell sublime, *L. × intermedia* 'Seal' is outstanding; *L.* 'Sawyers' has outsize, tapered flower spikes. Once you have a few varieties, inevitably you will want more. The frost-tender lavenders that you can grow in pots and bring under glass in winter have especially beautiful, intensely aromatic foliage; the leaves of *L. dentata* are finely scrolled, those of *L. pinnata* are fern-like. Both plants often flower through winter and spring.

How to Grow Lavender

Like most Mediterranean plants, lavenders do not need fertilizer, which will only stimulate leaf growth and weaken the fragrance. Plant young plants 60cm/24in apart, or for a hedge, 30–45cm/12–18in apart, in an open, sunny site, with well-drained soil. Given the right soil conditions, they will flower in semi-shade. Cut back faded flower stems, and shape up the bush in spring, but do not cut into the old wood, because it will not reshoot.

Above left: *This garden of only lavender and olive trees was created in a Tuscan vineyard.*

Above right: *For drying, bunches of lavender should be hung up before the florets are fully open.*

Where to Plant Lavender

Plant lavenders where you will brush past them to release their fragrance, as a hedge or path edging. Grow them alongside cistus and rosemary, as they grow in the wild; site them at the foot of pergolas or on either side of a garden seat, in the ground or massed in outside pots.

How to Harvest Lavender

The big dilemma – aside from deciding which to plant – is when to cut the flowers. The volatile oils are at their peak just before the flowers come into full bloom, so pick at that point for the best scent. Alternatively, enjoy the flowers on the bush, and cut the stalks after flowering..

What can you do with the cut flowers? Lavender bags and bottles – where the stems of a bunch of lavender are folded over to encase the flowers – can be tucked in between the folds of linen or lingerie. Lavender stalks can be strewn on to the car floor, as a traffic stressbeater. Jam a huge bunch of lavender stems tightly into a large terracotta pot to enjoy through winter, as a fragrant reminder of summer. Lavender essential oil is widely used in aromatherapy for its ability to calm as well as revive the spirits. Equally beneficial is simply to roll the lavender spike between your fingers and breathe deeply.

seaside dwellers

Mediterranean maritime plants

Why grow seaside plants? Because they thrive in the typical conditions of the Mediterranean garden: poor, freely draining soil, little rain. Because they are tough survivors that have to endure drought, fierce gales and salt sprays, so you know they will be fine in your plot, especially if you are on an exposed hillside or in a high rise. Last but not least, because many of them are little gems.

You probably already have one or two seaside-dwellers growing in your garden, without realizing it: rosemary – *Rosmarinus* – translates from the Latin as "dew of the sea", because it inhabits sand dunes and maritime rocks. The natural home of *Convolvulus cneorum*, with silver leaves and white trumpet flowers, is on calcareous rocks, close to the shore. The following are a few other seaside stalwarts you might not be familiar with but might consider growing.

Convolvulus cneorum.

Armeria maritima.

ARMERIA MARITIMA ***
Thrift's low-growing, tussocky shape enables it to resist whipping clifftop winds, and the needle-like leaves have little surface area from which water will evaporate, so they are well-equipped to withstand drought. The drumstick flowers produced in late spring through summer are pink, sometimes white, but *Armeria maritima* 'Corsica' has flowers in a striking brick red.

ERYNGIUM MARITIMUM ***
The sea holly has a long, questing tap root and spiny foliage to keep in moisture. It is a handsome perennial plant with sprawling stems, prickly blue grey leaves and powder blue cone flowers set in holly-shaped bracts, like silver collars.

Eryngium maritimum.

Glaucium flavum.

GLAUCIUM FLAVUM ***

The flowers of the horned poppy are papery yellow, and last only a day or so; the seed capsules form very long, horn-like pods that are the same grey green as the fleshy, frilly leaves. This poppy's tap root can forage for fresh water for over 2m/6ft. A biennial, *Glaucium flavum* is a habitué of dunes and sandy beaches. Orange-flowered *Glaucium flavum*. f. *fulvum* is a flamboyant close relative.

Myrtus communis *ssp.* tarentina.

Lampranthus.

LAMPRANTHUS FT

This emigré from South Africa is widely planted in gardens in the Mediterranean and has naturalized in rocky, coastal habitats. There are many species and hybrids, but all these succulents produce trailing stems with succulent leaves, and, at their tips, raffia-like daisy flowers in the brightest of shades from white to purple. Some lampranthus may tolerate light frost, but will rot in cold, damp conditions, so siting them in crevices of rocks on a slope is ideal. Otherwise, grow them in containers.

LAVATERA MARITIMA **

Sea mallow grows in rocky, coastal habitats as well as inland. The leaves are grey green and the small flowers flushed pink. It is more compact than most lavateras at 1m/39in tall.

MYRTUS COMMUNIS SSP. TARENTINA **

The tarentine myrtle grows mainly in coastal habitats, and is a smaller version of the better known myrtle bush, growing to 2m/6ft. The aromatic leaves are pointed at the tips, and, like its relative, the flowers are white and fragrant, followed by black fruits. As this shrub is not fully frost hardy, grow it against a warm, sheltered wall, or in a container.

Lavatera maritima.

TAMARIX ***

Find the elegant tamarisk tree by a riverbank, stream or coastal marsh; the feathery plumes of flowers and purple bark make it an asset to your garden. *Tamarix gallica* grows to about 2m/6ft tall, is deciduous, and has small, blue grey leaves and pink flower racemes in summer. *Tamarix tetrandra* and *africana* flowers in early summer, while *Tamarix ramosissima* flowers in late summer.

Tamarix africana.

non-stop fireworks

Mediterranean bulbs

Bulbs are big in the Mediterranean, in more ways than one. Many of the species tulips, narcissi, grape hyacinths, crocuses and other bulbous beauties that we grow in our gardens originate in the Mediterranean. They flower there in the cool and moist autumn, late winter or spring, and retreat underground as a swollen bulb, corm, rhizome or tuber during the summer drought. Perhaps it is because Greece has the driest climate in Europe that so many of its endemic wildflowers are bulbs.

The choice offered to the gardener is vast, so the suggestions on these pages cover just some of the most sumptuous, as well as the most foolproof and frost hardy. In a more moderate climate Mediterranean bulbs will flower a little later, so that some of the spring-flowering bulbs bloom in a cooler garden in summer.

Plant bulbs in drifts, clumps, and in meandering rivers in and around shrubs. It is a good idea to mark the spot with an indelible marker tag, or the chances are that you

Left: *The rich purple blooms of* Anemone coronaria *nestle among* Coronilla, *making a sultry combination.*

Right: *Sugar pink* Tulipa saxatilis *and* Tulipa clusiana *var.* chrysantha *make bright splashes amongst the euphorbia.*

will dig them up inadvertently. Take your pick from statuesque ornamental onions with purple puffball heads, exuberant asphodels with flower spikes the colour of sunshine, magenta spears of wild gladioli, classic white Madonna lilies and striped and checkered fritillaries. Or throw caution to the wind, grow them all, and prepare for non-stop fireworks.

PLANTING POINTERS
- Use species bulbs to mingle with Mediterranean plants, and chunkier hybrids for containers.
- Plant some bulbs in black plastic pots so that you can sink them into the ground to fill gaps.

How to Plant Bulbs

The key to success is to give bulbs free-draining soil with plenty of grit or gravel to open the texture; you will lose them if they sit in water. A mulch of grit or gravel will increase their hardiness, too. Most Mediterranean bulbs appreciate a sunny spot where they can settle and, in the case of crocuses and tulips, spread their petals wide. Bury bulbs at three times their own depth, but plant iris rhizomes just proud of the soil surface so that they get a good baking. After flowering, resist the temptation to cut down their foliage, and leave them in the ground to naturalize, dividing clumps just before the leaves die down as they become congested.

What to Plant When

Most bulbs should be planted in the autumn, earlier rather than later. Asphodel tubers can be planted in spring or autumn, as soon as you get them. Madonna lilies must be planted in late summer so that there is time for their foliage rosettes to grow before winter. The bulbs of *Sternbergia lutea* should be planted in the autumn, but you may have to wait a year or two for them to flower.

Below right: *The pure white Madonna lily provides cool respite from hot summer colour.*

Below left: *Spikes of yellow asphodel and cerise gladioli add sizzle to the garden in summer.*

Above: *Two-tone grape hyacinth* Muscari latifolium *provides shots of blue early in the gardening year.*

Buying Species Bulbs

Many species of Mediterranean bulbs are endangered, not least by illegal harvesting for sale to gardeners. When you buy species bulbs, check with the nursery or garden centre that they have come from a reputable source and have been propagated from cultivated stocks, not collected from the wild.

Bulbs for spring to early summer

Amongst the evergreens that form the permanent backbone of the Mediterranean garden, in spaces and slivers of gravel, plant paintbox-bright bulbs to pop up in profusion every spring. All are fully hardy.

Plant wisely and you can have a continuous flow of colour and excitement that leads deftly from spring into summer.

Right: Tulipa clusiana *var.* chrysantha *and grape hyacinth amongst the lime-green heads of* Euphorbia myrsinites.

Nectaroscordum siculum.

ALLIUM

So many alliums, so little space. The decorative side of the onion family produces wands of puffball flowers that add immense style to the garden. Early on, *Allium moly* produces starry yellow flower clusters on modest 25cm/10in stems. It naturalizes readily, or spreads like weeds, depending how you feel about it, and prefers shade. *Allium roseum*, the rosy garlic, has dainty flower umbels of pale pink on stems up to 35cm/14in high. *Nectaroscordum siculum* is a gorgeous allium that flowers as summer starts. It has spider-like flowerheads on stems 1m/39in tall, and a large rosette of foliage. The individual flowers are streaked rose and green. As they fade they form wondrous seedheads.

Allium moly.

Anemone coronaria.

Crocus ancyrensis.

Fritillaria persica.

ANEMONE

These flowers of Greek mythology transform the Mediterranean landscape in spring; plant them to create smaller-scale pools of colour in your garden. The Greek windflower, *Anemone blanda*, opens its lavender blue petals – sometimes white – wide to the spring sun, high up in the mountains. The tubers will be equally content in your garden; plant them in open gravel spaces in generous drifts.

In olive groves and vineyards, fields and waysides, the crown anemone, *Anemone coronaria*, is everywhere in the Mediterranean in spring. The lime green, finely cut foliage emerges first, followed by the flowers, which make welcome dollops of paintbox colours – scarlet, blue, purple – and look spectacular alongside yellow flowers, such as *Alyssum saxatile* or coronilla. The tubers can also be planted in broad grit-topped bulb bowls.

CROCUS

Crocuses are usually confined to small areas throughout the Mediterranean; smaller than the Dutch hybrids, what they lack in size, they make up for in beauty as well as quantity. All are suited to containers. *Crocus ancyrensis*, from Turkey, has rich, golden yellow flowers that are welcome rays of sunshine in early spring; for containers, choose the cultivar 'Golden Bunch' which supplies several flowers per stem, more than the species. In Corsica and Sardinia, the purple flowers of *Crocus corsicus* bloom on stony pastures. *Crocus etruscus* is a simple, one-note lavender crocus with a yellow throat, from Tuscany. *Crocus minimus* is predominantly lavender, but the outer petals have exquisite deepest purple featherings on white.

Fritillaria acmopetala.

CYCLAMEN

Often growing out of rock fissures and at the base of trees, cyclamen thrive in partly shaded sites, producing marbled, heart-shaped leaves before the coiled stems spring out, topped with butterfly flowers of magenta, rose pink or white. *Cyclamen repandum* is a spring-flowering woodlander with scented magenta flowers and plain or patterned leaves. Plant the tubers no more than 2.5cm/1in deep.

FRITILLARIA

Greece alone has 17 species of fritillaries, none of which are easy to grow in gardens. Light shade suits them best, such as that beneath Spanish broom. *Fritillaria acmopetala* has beautiful green flowerheads with carmine markings dangling from 45cm/18in stems. It is best appreciated in pots. The stunning dusky chocolate brown bellflowers of *Fritillaria persica* are borne on a glaucous blue stem about 1m/39in tall, with handsome leaves. Somehow its beauty is enhanced by the fact that it does not choose to make an appearance every spring. Place the bulbs sideways when you plant, and keep your fingers crossed.

HERMODACTYLUS TUBEROSUS

The finger-like rhizomes give this plant its name, 'Finger of Hermes'. Not surprisingly, it grows throughout Greece on stony soil and blooms in early spring. Known as the widow iris, it is sinister, beautiful and fleeting, with a flower of translucent green inner petals and black velvet outer petals on a 30cm/12in stem. Divide established clumps in autumn.

IRIS

Rhizomous irises should have their rhizomes planted shallowly so that the top edges are exposed to the sun. *Iris attica* is a small, heartbreaker iris with papery, buff-coloured petals that need cloching to protect them from heavy rain. This is one for a trough or container.

MUSCARI

Grape hyacinths grow freely in the Mediterranean and, some might say, a little too freely in the garden, but they are invaluable for supplying a splash of bright blue in spring and

Hermodactylus tuberosus.

are terrific in containers, too. *Muscari armeniacum*, the Armenian grape hyacinth, supplies pyramidal spikes of cheery powder blue; plant them to bloom alongside the lime green frothy flowerheads of *Euphorbia myrsinite*s and bright red *Anemone coronaria*, or scarlet tulips such as *Tulipa linifolia*. *Muscari latifolium* has a flower of inkiest blue topped with a tuft of powder blue; plant it at the

front of beds or in pots where the two-tone effect can be admired. *Muscari neglectum* is the common grape hyacinth of the Mediterranean region. It is similar to *M. armeniacum*, but the flowers are nearer to navy blue.

NARCISSUS

Although the narcissus sometimes leans over a stream to mimic the beautiful Narcissus who fell in love with his reflection, some narcissi do thrive in somewhat drier places. The common name "hoop petticoat" best describes the golden flowers of *Narcissus bulbocodium*, usually seen on mountain pastures. Only 15cm/6in tall, it does best with some moisture, so incorporate organic matter into the planting hole. Once established, it will naturalize. *Narcissus tazetta* is a native of meadows and pastures with several creamy fragrant flowers per 30cm/12in stem. It is said to be tender, but survives well under a thick gravel coverlet, in the shelter of a warm wall. The taller hybrid 'Paper White' is better known.

Iris attica.

Muscari latifolium.

Narcissus bulbocodium.

Ornithogalum nutans.

ORNITHOGALUM

Over 20 species grow in the Mediterranean, confusingly all called the Star of Bethlehem. *Ornithogalum nutans* is more of a star than some of the others, with green-streaked silvery white flowers, about a dozen along each upright stem, 25cm/10in tall. Flowering in late spring, it is best seen in isolation and is suited to growing in partial shade.

TULIPA

Species tulips are daintier than hybrids, and many of them have beautiful, subtle markings. An immigrant from Iran, the lady tulip, *Tulipa clusiana*, has naturalized in much of the Mediterranean and is easily distinguished by her delectable white outer petals suffused with red stripes. She looks lovely popping up amongst prostrate rosemary. *T. clusiana* var. *chrysantha* has a yellow base, striking with red, while the hybrid 'Cynthia' has dainty striped lemon and pink flowers. *Tulipa linifolia* has shimmering vermilion flowers, which open to a wide triangle; it is terrific solo in the ground, or in containers, and grows up to 20cm/8in. Big, bold and beautiful, the wild orange *Tulipa orphanidea* has flame petals licked with lemon and green that curl outwards at the tips and look wonderful with grey shrubs. It grows up to 30cm/12in high.

The bowl-like, sugar pink flowers of the Cretan *Tulipa saxatilis* have hidden depths; namely, a large central dollop of egg yolk yellow, which is

Tulipa orphanidea.

revealed when they open their petals to greet the sun. Plant with a shrubby backdrop of silver, grey or lime green. *Tulipa saxatilis* Bakeri is very similar, but the flowers are a little smaller. *Tulipa sylvestris*, the wild tulip of the Mediterranean, is the most widespread, and has yellow flowers flushed with red and green. Its height is variable, up to 45cm/18in. It looks best in natural-looking drifts.

Tulipa clusiana *var.* chrysantha.

Tulipa saxatilis.

Tulipa sylvestris.

Bulbs for summer to autumn

Just planting different kinds of alliums alone will give you plenty of excitement in the Mediterranean garden in summer. Add lilies, asphodels and other key players, in abundance, and you will have a wonderful, heady mix of shooting stars for months ahead. Again, all the bulbs listed below are fully hardy.

Right: Byzantine gladioli and Cistus purpureus *make an audacious colour combination in the Mediterranean garden in summer.*

Allium nigrum.

ALLIUM
The wild leek of wasteland and roadsides, *Allium ampeloprasum*, is compulsory for its dramatic presence. The pink heads shoot skywards to bowl about on flexible but sturdy 150cm/5ft stems. The broad leaves start to die down as the flower develops in late summer. Like many alliums, the flowers fade on the stem to add structure to the garden in winter. *Allium nigrum* makes an unusual white puffball with green centres to each flower, 1m/39in high: good as a crowd.

The luscious blackcurrant puffballs of *Allium atropurpureum*, on 1m/39in stems, are striking alongside silver and grey foliage, while *Allium schubertii* looks like a firework caught in mid-explosion: it

Allium atropurpureum.

Allium sphaerocephalon.

Asphodelus lutea.

Gladiolus.

is amazing to think that these outsize, sputnik-like heads are natural, not man-made. This one is best in front of a bed as its stems are short. It dries well. *Allium sphaerocephalon* is one of the most useful summer-flowering bulbs because the foliage takes up no space, and the claret-coloured lozenge heads – they start out lime green – are beauties in their own right, yet mesh with everything. It is especially good with grey foliage, and fun with steely blue *Echinops* and *Eryngium*, flowering in late summer.
Nectaroscordum siculum has spider-like flower clusters on 90cm/36in stems.

ASPHODEL
Asphodelus lutea, Jacob's rod, grows in scrub and rocky meadows throughout the Mediterranean. The tuberous root produces whorls of grey green grass-like leaves and 1m/39in fat spikes of sunshine yellow star-shaped flowers that form round, shiny green seed pods. Wonderfully showy, it is too decorative to miss out on, and looks absolutely sensational with pink cistus. *Asphodelus albus* has elegant spires of starry white flowers streaked with green, and can reach 120cm/48in.

CYCLAMEN HEDERIFOLIUM
An autumn-flowering *maquis* plant for semi-shade, ideal under trees, this cyclamen is well known as a garden plant. The beautifully marked pink flowers have a purplish blotch at their base, and the heart-shaped leaves are often marbled and variegated. Plant no more than 2.5cm/1in deep.

GLADIOLUS
The wild gladioli of the Mediterranean are very different to the cultivated hybrids. These have the same sword-like leaves and flower habit, but are all exquisite shades of rose pink to rich magenta, and have a daintier beauty. *Gladiolus communis* ssp. *byzantinus* is the one species that is readily available in cultivation. The byzantine gladiolus grows wild in scrub, sometimes with fan palms as neighbours: cistus makes a slightly less exotic but sizzling accompaniment, although a background of evergreen shrubs show it off to perfection. The robust magenta stems can reach 1m/39in. Species gladioli flower in early summer.

Allium schubertii.

Cyclamen hederifolium.

Iris pallida *ssp.* pallida.

Iris germanica.

Iris foetidissima.

IRIS

The tall, bearded iris is widely grown in many Mediterranean gardens, and looks beautiful in extravagant drifts, as well as in groups of three or five to admire at close quarters. Plant the rhizomes close to the soil's surface, facing the sun, so they can be baked. Lift and divide after flowering when the clumps become overcrowded.

Iris foetidissima is known as the stinking iris because the evergreen leaves smell nasty when crushed. The dull purple or yellow flowers are modest, but there are two reasons for growing this iris of scrub and hedgerow: it thrives in shade and produces vibrant berries in autumn.

Iris germanica, the German iris, has been cultivated for centuries and frequents rocky ground, roadsides and field margins. The pale violet flowers have a central golden velvet beard, and grow in groups of three or four on branching stems up to 90cm/36in, from a typical fan of broad iris leaves. The variant, 'Florentina', has grey white flowers, and is commercially grown in Italy and France, where the rhizomes are used to produce orris root for the perfume industry.

Handsome, broad foliage fans of grey green are sufficient reason to grow *Iris pallida* ssp. *pallida.* The scented flowers are a stunning lavender blue, on stems of up to 90cm/36in.

Iris germanica *garden cultivars.*

Iris florentina alba.

Lilium candidum.

LILIUM

It is little wonder that the perfect Madonna lily *Lilium candidum* was the symbol of grace and purity for the ancient Greeks and Romans. It has glossy leaves, white trumpet flowers, golden stamens and the most wonderful perfume. Unlike other lilies, the Madonna lily bulb must be planted close to the surface of the soil, in late summer. It is not suitable for containers.

Lilium martagon.

Each 120cm/48in stem of the graceful Turk's cap lily *Lilium martagon* has a candelabrum of swept-back drooping flowers in spotted, dull pink. Though not typically Mediterranean, it is a good European lily, which will work well in most gardens as it it is suitable for either full sun or dappled shade. The variant var. *album* has white flowers, so it is useful where you want to brighten up a dull corner.

ORNITHOGALUM NARBONENSE

This summer-flowering Star of Bethlehem can reach an imposing 60cm/24in. The raceme holds many star-shaped white flowers; each petal is streaked with green. It is best in full sun, and grows so profusely on hillsides in Israel that its white flowers *en masse* look like bird droppings, hence its un-flattering biblical name, 'dove's dung'. Do not let this put you off; this bulb is a beauty.

STERNBERGIA LUTEA

Rather like a large golden crocus reaching up to 20cm/8in, *Sternbergia's* funnel flowers appear after the first autumn rains in scrub and on hillsides. Plant shallowly and leave undisturbed to form clumps over time.

And one stalwart for flowering in winter ...

Plant *Iris stylosa*, the Algerian iris, at the foot of a warm wall in the poorest, rubbly soil and it will reward you with small but beautiful mauve, scented iris flowers in the dead of winter. Consider it an essential to remind you of the delights to come in the following year.

Ornithogalum narbonense.

Iris stylosa.

Sizzling succulents

Succulents are spectacular. If you need convincing, witness the spiky agaves that grow like huge starfish along roadsides, on rocky slopes and in parks throughout the Mediterranean. Marvel at the sheets of fleshy lampranthus, their trailing stems finished with raffia-type shiny flowers, that grow rampantly on coastal dunes. And blink with disbelief at the aeonium, like a miniature palm tree, that has naturalized throughout the Mediterranean and is occasionally an extraordinary shade of shiny deep chocolate. If you cannot see these plants and other succulents growing *in situ*, look for them small-scale at your local garden centre, for they are just as weird and wonderful in containers. Curiosity value aside, there is another terrific reason for becoming familiar with a few members of this vast family:

succulents are the ultimate low-maintenance plants, ideal for windowboxes and pots that have a forgetful owner. Consider the sempervivums that cover the roofs of whitewashed houses in Greece, where they happily thrive for months without any water at all.

The collective name of this varied plant group gives the clue to their drought-busting characteristic: namely, fleshy leaves – and sometimes thick stems and roots – that hold their own water reservoir. Their distinctive hard, sometimes waxy skins actually seal in water. If your garden gets frost, then grow agaves in pots, and sink them into the ground, mulching over with gravel so that only you know the truth. At the end of summer, they can be pulled out to be overwintered in the house or under glass.

Above: *The chunky glaucous green rosettes of echeveria growing amongst yellow buttonheads of santolina.*

Left: *Echeverias produce extraordinary yellow flower spikes and seem to survive on nothing but air.*

Above: *Mahogany coloured aeoniums make a striking contrast with another succulent, lampranthus.*

Below: *A fabulous landscape, like a setting for a sci-fi movie, displays a broad range of succulents.*

Above: *Echeverias growing out of the nooks and crannies of an old stone archway.*

CONTAINER SUCCULENTS

Seek out novel varieties of succulents and plant them in containers. If you initially have trouble finding suitable plants then look in the garden centre or plant nursery under the category of miniature cactus gardens, where they may be planted in groups in one pot. It is worth prising out the small plants and growing them on in individual pots. Never mind the names, just consider their peculiar and sometimes ravishing demeanours, especially when the fleshy rosettes throw out sugar pink stems decked with flower clusters of yellow, pink and tangerine, like day-glo candy. Use them to add panache and spark to your container displays; the soft greys and milky greens of the foliage are a good foil for bright and brash pelargoniums.

Succulents are used to extreme temperatures – they hail from desert regions where the days are scorching and the nights are bitterly cold – but they will not tolerate frost, and excess water can make them rot. So bring the plants indoors in the autumn, and take cuttings as insurance.

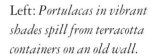

Left: *Portulacas in vibrant shades spill from terracotta containers on an old wall.*

PROPAGATING SUCCULENTS

Be warned: succulents are addictive, especially when you discover how easy they are to propagate. Agaves and aloes produce babies around their base that can be potted up; other succulents produce baby rosettes that can be gently prised out of the compost (soil mix) and grown on. You need only chop the heads off multi-branched aeoniums – leave a small stem attached, and allow the cut to callus over – and push them into the compost for them to take root. Use special cactus compost, because it is exceptionally free-draining, and a cactus feed that has suitable nutrients. Welcome to a whole new world of plant fascination.

Right: *Aeoniums and echeverias could not be easier to propagate: just cut their heads off.*

Above: *In a frost-free garden, the rose pink daisy flowers of beach aster mingle with echeveria rosettes.*

Above: *The diverse shapes, textures and unique flowers of succulents are displayed on a rooftop in the Scilly Isles.*

Right: *The near-black succulent* Aeonium 'Zwartkop' *produces starry yellow flowers from its rosettes, which die afterwards.*

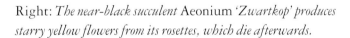

Above: *Different colours of portulaca are planted in each pot of this four-in-one container.*

Above: *Overlooked by* Agave americana '*Variegata*', *baby agaves and an echeveria grow out of a strawberry pot.*

Herbs, fruit and vegetables

Reap a rich harvest year-round with aromatic

Mediterranean herbs; savour baby purple

edible plants

aubergines (eggplants), glossy red peppers

and speckled firetongue beans. And in your

aromatic herbs

bountiful Mediterranean potager, pick

lemons   straight

from the tree.

sun-ripened

The fruits of the Mediterranean garden

The beauty of sun-ripened, home-grown produce is that it needs little fuss or embellishment; how can you improve on perfection? If your idea of *al fresco* eating is to take things easy, you'll find it blissful to be able to pick a few leaves, herbs and vegetables from your garden and present them at table, with only fresh lemons and green olive oil necessary to heighten their wonderful tastes and aromas.

The produce in this chapter, however, will give you the basics for many Mediterranean dishes, from simple roasted peppers to the Provençal tian of baked courgettes (zucchini) or *chichoumeille* of aubergines (eggplant), onions and tomatoes, if that should tickle your tastebuds. Growing Mediterranean herbs will provide flavoursome, fresh oregano for Greek salad, and the equally essential basil – in three different varieties, no less – to accompany your own home-grown tomatoes. Using the freshest flat-leaf parsley to make *gremolata*, the Italian paste of finely chopped

parsley, lemon rind and garlic, to dollop on just about everything, justifies growing this elegant leaf in a large trough or bucket.

You may not have enough olives to warrant curing them, but you can chop up your own fresh thyme, rosemary and lemon rind to marinate good shop-bought olives. And even if your vine-in-a-pot doesn't produce grapes, you can use the leaves as a green platter for goat's cheese or, blanched, to wrap around pine nuts, raisins and rice for Greek *dolmades*. Ripe tomatoes – the ones ripening on the vine, naturally – are requisites for the delicious Tuscan salad *panzanella*, a variable mix of stale soaked bread, ripe chopped tomatoes, red onions, celery and basil, dressed with olive oil and wine vinegar. Or you could bake them Provençal-style by sprinkling them with thyme, parsley and breadcrumbs, drizzled with olive oil, in a hot oven till soft and brown on top. Courgettes

Left: *Eating* al fresco *is a long, leisurely and pleasurable affair.*

Above: *Greek salad of feta cheese liberally scattered with home-grown oregano.*

Above: *Tomatoes, mozzarella, olives, anchovies and peppers make a feisty, flavourful summer salad.*

Below: *Sage, rosemary, oregano and thyme are key Mediterranean herbs.*

Above: *Sumptuous Mediterranean fruits and vegetables form the basis of easy, delicious outdoor eating.*

picked straight from the plant are tender enough to slice thinly and eat raw, or you could dunk the flowers in batter and fry them in olive oil, as the Italians do.

Peppery rocket (arugula) leaves with olive oil and a shaving of parmesan or pecorino cheese make a superb salad, Tuscan-style. *Mesclun* is the loose leaf mix that originates from Provence, traditionally for winter growing in the south: it is equally easy to grow from seed scattered on the ground or in a container. I grow *mesclun* muddled up with the Italian mix *saladisi*, and serve Greek *gazpacho* alongside *salade niçoise*. Why be precious about separating *mezze* from *antipasto*, or preventing the tastes of the convivial *la merenda* from merging with crudités and aïoli? We can dip into the whole rich and varied cuisine of the Mediterranean, gathering together the tastes and ideas of different countries and regions all on one table.

hillside produce

Kitchen herbs

In the Mediterranean, scrub and hillside produce so much rosemary, sage, thyme, oregano and winter savory that many people pick what they need from these shrubby native evergreens, and grow herbs in their gardens that are best in pots, such as basil, mint and coriander (cilantro). When we grow these aromatic herbs in our gardens, we need to re-create the dry, stony habitat in which they grow, because it is in these harsh conditions that they produce the highest concentrations of essential oils and therefore provide the most flavour. As the backbone to the Mediterranean garden, all of these herbs, with the exception of mint, which needs moister conditions, and the restraints of a container, need planting in sharply drained soil.

The following list includes the key herbs that grow in the Mediterranean, and those that are most widely used in cooking. All can be propagated from cuttings.

Right: A large patch of rosemary grows outside a house in Tuscany, so that clippings for the kitchen are just a step away.

Lemon thyme.

THYME ***
Probably the most widely used herb, and certainly one of the most freely available, thyme grows all over the *garrigue*. The wild *Thymus vulgaris* forms a small, stubbly bush, and is called *farigoule* in Provence, where it is used to add warm, earthy flavour to casseroles and grills, and rubbed into lamb and chicken before cooking. *Riquiqui* – the Provençal thyme digestif – is made from thyme flowers infused in sugar and vodka for many weeks; you can do the same with sage, too. Creeping thyme, *Thymus serpyllum*, is a hillside habitué, and has many garden cultivars; it has a good perfume, so is used in infusions. Lemon thyme is wonderful rubbed over chicken before cooking, but then so is orange thyme.

Winter savory growing wild.

Prostrate rosemary.

Wild oregano.

Moroccan mint.

ROSEMARY **

The freeform bush *Rosmarinus officinalis* grows on sand dunes as well as in scrub and woodland. It has cultivars with different flowers, but there is also the better-behaved 'Miss Jessopp's Upright', and the Prostratus Group of tumbling rosemaries, ideal for growing over low walls or banks, and for containers. This last group is variable; not all are fully frost hardy, and they need a sheltered site. For the deepest blue flowers grow *R. officinalis* 'Fota Blue'. Rosemary is widely used in cooking, especially as a marinade for meat and fish, and also with courgettes (zucchini) and tomatoes. It is a classic partner to garlic for roast lamb and chicken.

OREGANO ***

Oregano gets its name from the Greek *origanon*, meaning "bitter herb". For their beauty, grow some of the decorative oreganos but for cooking, grow *Origanum vulgare* from the mountains of Greece. You might know it better as wild marjoram. Plant gold varieties in a little shade as they can scorch in full sun. Oregano is excellent with tomato dishes, aubergines (eggplant), pizza, salads and stews, and is good dried.

WINTER SAVORY ***

Satureja montana grows on rocky slopes and has thyme-like leaves with small white and pink flowers. A partial evergreen, it has the bonus of providing fresh growth through the beginning of winter, and it is close enough in aroma to thyme to be used as a substitute; in southern Italy both thyme and savory are called *timo*. Winter savory is used to flavour grilled lamb and fish, and cooked with beans and pulses, as it aids digestion.

SAGE ***

Salvia officinalis, common sage, is native to the northern Mediterranean, and grows in scrub and stony pastures. Varieties include decorative purple foliage and tricolour foliage, which is less vigorous, as well as narrow-leaved, highly aromatic Spanish sage; all

Sage flowers.

produce decorative pink or mauve flower spikes. Sage is mostly used in Tuscan dishes, especially fried with liver. In Provence, it is the main flavouring in *aigo bouido* – "life saver" – the health-giving soup simmered with garlic cloves. Sage was the tisane of the ancient Greeks, and it is still valued today as a medicinal plant.

MINT ***

Mentha spicata is the spearmint that grows in damp habitats and ditches as well as in gardens, but the variety 'Moroccan' is best for cooking, and of course for Moroccan mint tea. Mint is used widely in Greece for cooking, chopped with other herbs to flavour fish dishes and stuffed vegetables; it is a great refresher with yogurt. Grow it from runners in a container in soil-based compost, and keep it watered.

BAY **

In contrast to the neatly clipped bushes and trees in gardens, *Laurus nobilis* can reach 10m/33ft in the wild, where it grows in rocky places and ravines. The berries were pounded with herbs to flavour ancient Roman dishes, but now it is the fragrant leaves that are torn into stocks and stews. The bay wreath today still represents glory and excellence.

seasonal sowing

Herbs to grow from seed

The herbs listed below are ones that can be grown from seed with ease, and that retain their aroma and flavour. These days it is possible to buy pots of herbs to put on your kitchen windowsill from the super-market, but they will not have the sturdiness or staying power of those that you grow yourself. Sowing instructions for each herb are detailed under their individual entry.

Right: Herbs that have been propagated the previous year are now ready for sale.

Above: Feathery green fennel.

FENNEL ***

In the south of France, fennel is the perennial substitute for the annual dill, more commonly grown in the north. The foliage of bronze and green fennel decorates the garden as well as providing stalks – dried – to scent the fire for grilled fish, and fragrant green stuffing for oily fish. The leaves can also be used for fish stews. Sow in spring in pots or plug trays, and plant out when large enough to handle. Fennel dies back in the winter and reshoots the following spring.

CORIANDER ***

Coriandrum sativum was a favourite herb of the ancient Romans, but is now used more in Greek cooking, especially in Cyprus. In the eastern Mediterranean, the fragrant leaves are added at the end of cooking spicy dishes; in France, they are known as Arab parsley; in America the leaves are known as cilantro. Sow direct in pots or into cell trays in spring, potting on. Keep cutting so you use the newest leaves, but make several sowings throughout summer, in semi-shade, to keep a constant supply.

Above: *Greek basil (left), Napolitano (centre), and Genovese (right).*

BASIL *

No self-respecting Mediterranean tomato is complete without the distinctive flavour of basil, even though it is an Indian native that was brought in by migrant tribes. Seed catalogues list many varieties, but the main types for Mediterranean cooking are these: the miniature fine-leaved basil widely grown in Greece on windowsills (to deter flies as well as for cooking), *Ocimum minimum*; the most common variety, 'Genovese', *Ocimum basilicum* 'Genovese', *O.b.* 'Napolitano', the wrinkly lettuce-leaved basil, which originates in Naples and is a staple of spaghetti sauce in the south. Basil is added to salads, grilled meat, vegetables and fish, to Provençal *pistou* – made with garlic, basil, hard cheese and olive oil – and to Italian *pesto* which is similar, but made with pine nuts. Both these sauces can be dolloped on to pasta, fish, soups and salads. The large leaves of Neapolitan basil are wrapped around slivers of Parmesan, and have a more aniseed taste. Basil needs sun and shelter to thrive, so sow it direct in pots (or sow it in cell trays, and pot on) and give it a hot spot on your terrace or windowsill. Keep picking leaves from the top to encourage new growth, water early in the day and do not overwater – basil's roots will not tolerate cold, damp conditions.

FLAT-LEAF PARSLEY ***

In Provence, parsley is the most commonly used of all herbs, finely chopped, in omelettes, sauce, meat and fish dishes, and sprinkled on to black olives. Italians use flat-leaf parsley, which has a better flavour than the curly kind, as an important ingredient rather than a fiddly garnish; try *gremolata*, the aromatic, punchy dressing made from chopped parsley, garlic and lemon rind. (Also, chew parsley after a meal to banish garlic on your breath, as the Italians do.)

Sow parsley in large, deep pots of soil-based compost in semi-shade, and keep cutting it to ensure a constant supply well into winter. Italian giant flat-leaf parsley, *Petroselinum crispum* var. *neapolitanum* (Italians call it *gigante*), which grows up to 70cm/28in, has a terrific flavour and is great torn into salads and pasta. I grow it unglamorously in a big metal bucket.

SUMMER SAVORY **

Satureja hortensis is called *sarriette* in Provence, but it is nicknamed "donkey's pepper" – *pebre d'ai* – because its peppery aroma makes grazing animals sneeze. An annual, it has a more delicate flavour than perennial winter savory but is used in similar dishes. Sow in cell trays in spring for potting on or planting directly into the ground; once in the garden, it will self-seed so you will have it year after year. Summer savory

Above: *A pot of flat-leaf parsley, left, and giant flat-leaf parsley, right.*

Making a Mediterranean herb garden

Herbal plants make up much of the *maquis,* so it follows that a large part of a native Mediterranean garden should be made up of these tough yet beautiful plants. In fact if you grew nothing but Mediterranean herbs, you would have a colourful, varied garden buzzing with colour that brings in bees and butterflies in droves. The intoxicating mix of resinous, aromatic fragrances emanating from the backbone plants of such a herb garden – curry-scented helichrysum, the sages, thymes, rosemary and all the different lavenders – has to be sniffed to be believed; in fact, you don't need to sniff, just stand well back and let the gorgeous *maquis* mix engulf you. Plant bulbs to shoot up in spring and summer around these textural domes and hummocks that, for the most part, stay in leaf through the year, and the picture is complete. And aside from owning

a beautiful, low-maintenance garden, you will be able to forage for herbs from large, billowing clumps instead of mean little pots, so you can harvest generous handfuls of aromatic foliage for most of the year.

To illustrate the point that a garden of only Mediterranean herbs is full of colour and vibrancy – and to offer an idea of the huge varieties of herbs, decorative and culinary, that are available – I made a Mediterranean herb border one spring. A year later, it was photographed: the pictures show how, given the right conditions, these plants spread and establish themselves in a very short time.

It suited me to make a raised bed against an old wall, because that location faced the sun for most of the day; Mediterranean herbs appreciate as much warmth and light as you can offer, as well as their usual requirement of gritty, well-drained soil.

Apart from placing prostrate – tumbling – rosemaries and spreading thymes along the front of the bed, so that they would spill over the edges as they grew, I put my faith in nature and planted without a plan, confident that all the colours – predominantly soft blue, pink and mauve flowers, silver, purple, green and grey foliage – would harmonize. After planting, I pushed a few borage seeds into the earth here and there, and sowed a few marigolds, both for their colour and their edible flowers. A miniature upright juniper was substituted for the fragrant wild juniper that grows in the mountains of Greece; the deep blue berries add flavouring to pork and wild boar, and are the base of the Italian liqueur *ginepro.*

The fruits of the pomegranate tree, regarded in mythology as a symbol of fertility, are classified as a herb because the juice has medicinal uses, as well as being made into the cordial, grenadine; the pretty tree in my Mediterranean bed does not produce fruits, but the burnished leaves and brilliant vermilion flowers are more than adequate to merit its inclusion.

Above: *This beautiful herb garden illustrates the broad varieties of texture and colour.*

Above: *The herb garden just planted in spring; compare with same view, fifteen months later, below right.*

Above: *Later the same summer, there was plenty of space for borage and the purple heads of* Allium sphaerocephalon.

Above: *Just four months after planting, the herbs are flowering and beginning to spread.*

Along the back wall, covered first with vine eyes and wires, I planted honeysuckle, purple-flowering *Clematis viticella*, the dusky-leaved vine *Vitis vinifera* 'Purpurea', and *Clematis cirrhosa*, the evergreen clematis of woods and *maquis*, for its honey-scented flowers in early spring. Somehow, shocking pink *Cistus crispus*, *Phlomis italica*, a cushion of golden broom, and the orange-flowered poppy *Glaucium flavum* f. *fulvum* crept in.

Cistus, it could be argued, qualifies as a herb because ladanum, the sticky gum secreted from the leaves of some varieties, has been used since ancient times as a key ingredient in perfume. *Glaucium flavum*, report the herbals, was once used as an eye medicine for animals. And although *Phlomis italica* makes the prettiest ornamental plant, in Greece the aromatic leaves are dried, and used to flavour casseroles.

Right: *A mere fifteen months after planting, the Mediterranean garden is established, and full of aromatic leaf and flower.*

Plants for a Mediterranean herb bed

This bed measures 5.4m/18ft in length, 2.2m/7ft in depth and is 60cm/24in high. Yours could be as small as a windowbox, or more than twice as large. To give you an idea of how much gravel you will need, the bed featured here took about two tons (or tonnes) as a soil texturizer and mulch to a depth of 5cm/2in.

The herbs you choose to grow may vary in variety and you may want a different balance for cooking. Plant them small, because herbs grow so quickly: plants in 8cm/3¼in pots are ideal. Where herbs are to form one large mat, plant three in a group, 23cm/9in apart, and leave about 30cm/12in between different herb species.

Angelica archangelica: angelica; ridged stems and expansive foliage reach 2m/6ft; produces large flower umbels in second year

Artemisia abrotanum: southernwood makes a 1m/39in bush of silvery-green, finely cut foliage

Artemisia dracunculus: French tarragon, dies down in winter

Foeniculum vulgare: green fennel; feathery, ferny fronds growing to 150cm/5ft

Foeniculum vulgare 'Purpureum': dark bronze fennel, up to 150cm/5ft

Helichrysum italicum: curry-scented, silver leaves with yellow flowers

Helichrysum italicum ssp. *microphyllum*: smaller version with filigree-like silver foliage

Hyssopus officinalis: blue-flowered hyssop (there are also white and pink forms)

Hyssopus officinalis ssp. *aristatus*: rock hyssop, compact variety, blue flowers

Lavandula x *intermedia* 'Seal': long stems and rich purple flowers, best fragrance

Lavandula 'Sawyers': grey leaves, large lavender blue tapered flowers

Lavandula stoechas: French lavender with purple flowers and grey green foliage

Lavandula stoechas ssp. *pedunculata*: French lavender with longer tufts, lighter flowers and pale apple-green foliage

Levisticum officinale: lovage; distinctive foliage like large celery stalks and leaves with a similar flavour

Origanum dictamnus: dittany of Crete; prostrate, woolly ice grey stems and foliage, hop-like pink flowers

Origanum vulgare: oregano, the wild form of marjoram; red-flushed green leaves, red stems, pinky purple flowers

Origanum vulgare 'Aureum': golden lime leaves, white flowers

Origanum vulgare ssp. *hirtum*: Greek oregano; white flowers

Phlomis italica: narrow-leaved Jerusalem sage; pale green, felty leaves; ice pink flowers in whorls

Rosmarinus officinalis: rosemary, pale blue flowers

Rosmarinus officinalis 'Fota Blue': the richest blue flowers

Rosmarinus officinalis 'Miss Jessopp's Upright': upright rosemary bush

Rosmarinus officinalis Prostratus Group: prostrate rosemary

Salvia lavandulifolia: narrow-leaved sage, lavender blue flowers

Salvia officinalis: pungent leaves, mauve flowers

Salvia officinalis 'Purpurascens': purple-leaved sage

Salvia officinalis 'Rosea': pretty lilac-pink flowers

Santolina chamaecyparissus: fine silvery foliage, yellow button flowers

Santolina rosmarinifolia ssp. *rosmarinifolia*: cotton lavender; green foliage, yellow button flowers

Satureja montana: winter savory

Satureja spicigera: creeping savory

Thymus x *citriodorus*: shrubby upright lemon-scented thyme

Thymus x 'Fragrantissimus': shrubby thyme with orange-scented foliage

Thymus 'Porlock': a tough, highly aromatic shrubby thyme

Thymus serpyllum: wild creeping thyme, pink flowers

Above: *The first summer, the Mediterranean herb garden is less exuberant, but still has charm.*

Above: *In the second summer alliums mix with French lavender,* Phlomis italica *and cistus, with a backdrop of honeysuckle.*

Above: *Content in the sharply drained, stony ground, the orange-horned poppy flowered right through the second summer.*

Above: *Fennel, sage in flower, hyssop and oregano in their second summer in the herb bed.*

Above: *A mass of shocking pink cistus packs a vibrant punch in early summer.*

HOW TO GET THE BEST FROM YOUR HERBS

- Keep clipping back herbs throughout the summer to use in the kitchen.
- Angelica and fennel make fine focal points; cut fennel back before it flowers or it will self-seed a little too prolifically.
- Watch out for herbs invading the space of others, or overshadowing them so that they do not receive their fair quota of sunlight; cut them back ruthlessly.
- Don't be tempted to grow mint in your Mediterranean herb bed: it spreads too fast, and prefers a richer, less dry soil. Instead grow it in pots.

Tactile thymes

Some herbs are so tactile they just ask to be stroked, and then, of course, they surrender their potent fragrances, leaving them on your skin like the finest aromatherapy treatment. Herbs are naturals for containers, not just for the cooking pot, but as decorative plants that you can cluster around a seat so that you can enjoy their volatile oils as you sit in the sun.

Consider growing compact marjoram, *Origanum vulgare* 'Compactum', as rounded cushions in large pots, one on either side of a seat. Lavenders, with their wonderfully textural foliage and flowers, are perfect for pots; grow a permanent bush of *Lavandula angustifolia* in an outsize terracotta pot, or several French lavenders, with their jaunty, tufted flowerheads that are impossible not to touch, in a smaller pot or ranged in a trough.

Group pots of rosemaries and lavenders together for a small-scale, sensual *maquis*. Grow several different varieties of thymes in pans, to snip for cooking, or simply just to run your hands over. Most tactile of all the thymes is *Thymus pseudolanuginosus*, whose common name translates more invitingly as woolly thyme, and that is just what it feels like.

Above: Origanum *makes an interesting textural container plant; keep it from flowering by strategic clipping.*

Above: *Make a small-scale* maquis *by grouping together rosemaries and lavenders, letting them grow wild and woolly.*

Above: *Different thymes make a marvellous patchwork of colour and texture, as these plants illustrate.*

A THYME GARDEN

One way of enjoying a patchwork carpet of various thymes is to make a thyme garden in a pot. Choose half a dozen small thyme plants, making the selection as diverse as possible. Fill a wide terracotta pot or pan, about 38cm/15cm diameter, with a free-draining planting mix consisting of half-and-half soil-based compost and grit. Include a thick layer of stone chippings in the base to improve the drainage further. Set a small sundial in the middle and surround it with the thymes, arranging them so that they contrast with each other. Top with a layer of grit or gravel and water thoroughly.

Above: *Small thyme plants in a variety of colours, forms and scents make a pretty composition in a container for a sunny patio or terrace, inviting you to run your hand over the contrasting textures. Position it so that the sundial tells the time.*

Above: *After a few weeks the plants have grown to fill the pot and spill over the edges. Keep cutting the thymes so that an upright variety does not take over, and allow them to flower to add even more variety to the planting.*

Vegetables from the Mediterranean garden

Plump fragrant tomatoes, sweet peppers and chilli peppers, glossy purple aubergines (eggplants), green as well as yellow courgettes (zucchini); growing just these few vegetables alone is enough to provide the basic ingredients for the celebrated Provençal dish, *ratatouille*. Because these vegetables need different conditions from Mediterranean natives, and so that you can keep a careful eye on them, it's advisable to grow them in containers. The speckled firetongue bean, too, grows beautifully in pots, providing novel crimson and cream speckled pods and purple flecked beans. Place your pots of vegetables in a sunny spot, and water them regularly and evenly. When they start to flower, give them a dilute solution of liquid tomato fertilizer or seaweed feed twice weekly. You will not get a huge harvest from your Mediterranean crops, but from summer to autumn there will be enough to provide a taste of the finest flavours of the Mediterranean.

TOMATO

For different tastes and uses, you could grow three different varieties:

The French large beef tomato variety 'Marmande' grows well outdoors (which is just as well, because bees are needed to pollinate it); 'Marmande' is a bush variety, and does not need pinching out or pruning.

Tall vine tomatoes 'San Marzano Lampadina' are very flavourful plum tomatoes; they are the kind used in southern Italy for bottling and drying.

Use small cherry tomatoes whole in salads and cooking. 'Tiny Tim', 'Tumbler' and 'Sweet 100' all produce sweet, tangy fruits. 'Phyra', a miniature bush tomato, is also worth growing for its grape-sized, pointed fruits that grow in long trails, rather like a wild tomato.

Left: *A hillside in the south of France presents the perfect location for a simple, small kitchen garden.*

Above: *The stems of these beefsteak tomatoes, growing in a sunny corner, are weighed down with the heaviness of the fruit.*

Left: *Plum tomatoes ripening on the vine have an enticing aroma as well as their famous luscious taste.*

AUBERGINE (EGGPLANT)

Despite their exotic appearance, aubergines are easy to grow, and need no staking. The variety 'Bambino' is good for containers because it is suitably small and because every part of the plant is so pretty: dusky, mauve-tinted leaves, lavender and gold flowers, and rich purple fruits not much bigger than a large egg. The plants should be transplanted individually into containers only when the roots fill the pot they are growing in, so that they are eventually planted into pots of about 18cm/7in diameter. Then grow them as you would tomatoes, giving them the sunniest patch available and watering and feeding them regularly. Alternatively, grow them in a conservatory or under glass.

Right: *Aubergines (eggplants) make the prettiest of container plants, producing lilac flowers as well as glossy purple fruits.*

'Thai' chilli pepper.

'Hungarian Hot Wax' chilli pepper.

'Cayenne' chilli pepper.

'Riot' chilli pepper.

PEPPER

These are among the easiest vegetables to grow, providing the most decorative of windowsill plants as well as prolific amounts of sweet bell peppers or fiery chillies for cooking. Choose a miniature bell pepper for pot-growing, such as 'Jingle Bells', 'Redskin' or 'Baby Belle'. The range of chilli or cayenne peppers – popular in the Basque country of south-western France – is huge, and varies greatly in shape as well as degrees of heat. Some can even be too hot to handle. Two to try are: 'Firecracker', cream, purple, red and orange cone fruits; and 'Apache', which has long slim fruits.

COURGETTE (ZUCCHINI)

The yellow *zucchini* are mellower and blander in flavour than the green, but their cheery colour is impossible to resist. Try the compact variety 'Gold Rush'. The beautiful blossoms of both colours, if they are to be stuffed or frittered, should be picked first thing in the morning. Courgettes grow well in containers, planted individually, but the pots need to be broad in order to accommodate foliage, flowers and fruit: at least 25cm/10in diameter.

Below: *Like all courgettes (zucchini), compact variety Gold Rush produces bright yellow flowers.*

Right: *The firetongue bean makes a novel patio plant that will shimmy up a long bamboo pole or simple wooden teepee.*

Below right : *Both the pod and bean are attractively mottled with distinctive crimson markings.*

FIRETONGUE BEAN

Borlotto 'Lingua di Fuoco' is the Italian name for these wonderfully ornamental pole beans that have excellent flavour and texture when dried or half dried (the pods may be eaten green too). One plant will be content to wrap itself around a tall bamboo pole in a deep 25cm/10in pot. To dry the beans, shell them and allow to dry naturally indoors in a warm environment, out of direct sunlight, before storing in jars.

Alternatively, grow 'Lingua di Fuoco' purely as an ornamental climber, and enjoy watching it scrambling up the side of a netted arch or wall.

potager

Growing vegetables from seed

Sowing from seed will not only produce the healthiest, most robust plants but also offer you a wider choice of the varieties you want. In spring, sow seeds for all your Mediterranean vegetables indoors in seed trays, approximately 2cm/¾in apart, lightly covered with compost (planting mix), or in individual plugs in cell trays. Use a suitable nutrient-free soilless compost mixed with Perlite to ensure free drainage. Place them in the warmth and darkness until they germinate. Courgette (zucchini) seeds and firetongue beans can be pushed 2cm/¾in deep into the compost direct into 8cm/3¼in pots, and potted on into containers as young plants.

CULTIVATION

Give these vegetables a sunny, sheltered corner on a patio or terrace, and water them first thing every morning; in very hot weather, you may need to water them in the evening, too. Courgettes (zucchini) are copious feeders, but tomatoes benefit from watering little and often; this is one case where overwatering produces fruit with little flavour, and can cause splitting of the skins. Bush varieties of tomatoes will need stout canes for support.

Water vegetables from above with a rose attached to the watering can, so that the leaves are refreshed; if they are in a dry, still spot they can suffer badly from red spider mite, but keeping the leaves sprayed with water will help prevent your plants succumbing to this irritating mite. Twice weekly, once the plants start to flower, give them a diluted feed of tomato fertilizer.

A TASTE OF THE MEDITERRANEAN

You could, of course, have an entire potager turned over to Mediterranean vegetables: Tuscan black cabbage 'Cavolo di Nero', 'Ratte' and 'Belle de Fontenay' potatoes, 'Violetto di Chioggia' purple artichokes, fat orange pumpkins, 'Romanesco' broccoli. You are limited only by the size of your plot, and your imagination.

POTTING-ON SEEDLINGS

When seedlings of tomatoes, aubergines (eggplants) and peppers show their first set of true leaves, they are ready to be moved to individual pots.

TOOLS AND MATERIALS
• seedlings
• 8cm/3¼in pots
• nutrient-free soilless

compost (planting mix)
• Perlite
• watering can

1 ◁ Tap the seed tray gently on the work surface so that the seedlings tip out, rather than trying to prise them out, which could damage the roots. If the roots are tangled together, gently pull them apart.

2 △ Fill an 8cm/3¼in pot with an equal mixture of compost (planting mix) and Perlite and tap it to settle it. Make a hole in the centre. Holding the seedling at the top of the stem, by the first leaf node, lower it into the hole.

3 △ Ease the compost around the seedling gently, without pushing it. Water in. When the seedlings have grown into sturdy small plants, re-pot and harden off gradually, placing them outdoors when all danger of frost is past.

SALAD VEGETABLES

Mediterraneans forage in woodland and wayside for tender shoots, roots and leaves such as wild asparagus, young dandelions and wild chicory to add to salads. In Tuscany nettles are even made into a kind of soufflé, called *sformato*. Here are a few suggestions for salad leaves and vegetables you can grow from seed in your own Mediterranean-type terrain. Borage looks good growing up amongst other plants, and can be used as a space filler, but the salad leaves should be grown in a separate patch of ground as although they are easy to grow, they will need diligent watering.

BORAGE

The young leaves of borage and its pretty blue star flowers are picked in Tuscany for salads, to add a light cucumber taste as well as decoration, and also for omelettes, stuffing ravioli and to make fritters. Sow borage seeds in spring by pushing them individually into the ground; once they flower, they will self-seed, but are easy to pull out if they grow too prolific.

ROCKET

Known as *rucola* in Italy, *roquette* in France, and arugula in America, this peppery leaf grows everywhere in the Mediterranean and is invaluable in livening up bland but prettier salad leaves such as lollo rosso, the frilly red, but flavourless, lettuce.

Wild rocket (arugula).

It also has a long growing season. Sow *Eruca sativa* in semi-dark, in seed trays or in open ground through spring, summer and into autumn in successive sowings; cover with a cloche for a supply early the next year. Keep harvesting the young leaves for the best flavour. Search out the wild variety, which has thicker, more serrated leaves, and more bite.

MIXED SALAD LEAVES

Mesclun, *misticanza* and *saladisi* are all regional variations on mixed leaves of varying textures (sometimes more varied than the taste). Depending on the seed mix, these can be a combination of any of the following: rocket (arugula), red and green oakleaf lettuce, romaine, chervil (Belgian endive), basil, purslane, radicchio, curly endive. The advantage of a loose leaf salad mix is that you cut it as you need it, and the leaves grow back to give you several clippings. You can either sow seed sparingly in a container or the open ground under glass from late winter, or in spring in the open ground.

GARLIC

Garlic is the staple of Provençal cooking, notably the garlic mayonnaise *aïoli*, called the "soul of the south", and *rouille*, the fiery sauce eaten in fish soup. Eaten raw, garlic is fierce, but cooked slowly, it becomes sweet and unctuous. Pink garlic is tastier than white, and keeps longer. From autumn to early spring, plant individual cloves in the ground, 3cm/1¼in deep, 15cm/6in apart, and harvest when the leaves turn yellow. Use the stalks to tie the heads in bunches and hang them to dry, Provençal-style. If kept in a cool, dry place they will last for several months.

Flowering borage.

Plaited garlic.

ancient plants

A trio of Mediterranean fruits to grow

In ancient Greece, the vine, olive and fig, together with a well of fresh water, were considered to be the basics of good living. And in the Bible, it is these same three that are mentioned throughout as symbols of peace and plenty, which is a sound reason to grow these ancient, beautiful plants in your own garden. Another is that, contrary to belief, they do not need heat to coax them through winter. Even if they do not fruit abundantly for you, the distinctive foliage is enough to evoke the spirit of the Mediterranean.

Olive grove in Umbria, Italy.

OLIVE **

Unless you have a very sheltered garden, in cooler climates olives are best grown in containers. Use a nutrient-rich compost (soil mix) such as John Innes No. 3, mixed with grit for drainage, and feed during the growing season with liquid seaweed fertilizer, which you can also use as a foliar feed. Olives are tougher than

Fruit-laden olive tree.

they are given credit for. It is not winter frost but prolonged wet that they cannot tolerate; many can stand temperatures of −10°C/14°F. Wrap the container itself in winter to protect the olive's roots, move the tree to the lee of a wall and mulch the compost with large cobbles that will keep off most of the winter rains.

When the tree blossoms in early summer and is covered with yellow pollen, spray the flowers with water to help the fruit to set. The olives are ready for picking six to eight months after the tree has blossomed, but they will need to be cured; raw, they taste terrible (the bitterness is slowly removed over weeks by soaking them in many changes of water). Prune to keep the tree in good shape.

Young olive tree in a pot.

Vitis vinifera 'Brant'.

Grapes in a Chianti vineyard.

Fig tree in a pot.

GRAPE ***

You can grow a vine against a warm wall, over an arbour to provide shade, or even in a large container, in which it will fruit and can also be kept under glass for winter. Use a nutrient-rich compost (soil mix) such as John Innes No. 3 for containers, with a handful of grit.

Plant in spring in well-drained soil with plenty of organic matter worked in, using vine eyes threaded with stout wire as wall support. Directly after planting, cut back the main stem to 60cm/24in and cut all sideshoots back to one bud. Mulch the roots and feed with general fertilizer to ensure good fruiting.

Tempting though it is, do not let your vine bear fruit for the first two years; it is more important to build up the framework. Pruning and training depend on the space you have allotted to it, but what is necessary is to prune the lateral shoots – the sideshoots from the main stem – back to the main stems each winter, so that growth is focused into a few buds. When the fruit starts to form, if it is grown for eating, the grapes themselves as well as the bunches should be thinned out to promote large fruits and discourage disease.

Vitis vinifera 'Brant' provides small, sweet purple bunches of dessert grapes and outstanding autumnal foliage tints. *Vitis labrusca* 'Concord' tolerates cold well and offers large bunches of black dessert grapes. For light and fruity wine, try the green grape vine 'Seyval Blanc'. 'Muscat of Alexandria', which has muscat-flavoured amber fruit, is ideal grown as a standard in a container, and is best brought in under glass or into a conservatory for the winter.

FIG ***

The best position for a fig tree is against a warm wall, facing the sun, and trained as a fan. You will need to restrict the fig's overactive roots: this is most easily achieved by making a "wall" of four paving stones, not smaller than 45cm/18in each, in a hole large enough to accommodate them; they should be just higher than the surface of the soil. Put plenty of stones or brick rubble at the base of the hole for drainage.

Water the fig well in the growing season and feed fortnightly with a high potash liquid feed. Pinching out occasional shoot tips in summer promotes bushiness, resulting in more fruit. If you want to cut out any old growth, the time to do it is in early spring.

Because they need to have their roots contained, figs are ideal for containers, and, being deciduous, can even sit in a shed through winter. Use John Innes No. 3 compost (soil mix) or a similar soil-based compost with added nutrients. Re-pot into a larger size container every autumn as the plant grows, but when it has reached the largest manageable size, take it out of the pot, tease away some of the soil from around the roots and cut them back by about 5cm/2in; repeat this root-prune every year, re-potting in fresh compost, to keep the tree within bounds.

Italians eat their first crop of figs in mid-June: these are the fruits that have ripened from the previous year, but the best crop is the one on the new shoots, from late August – these are smaller and sweeter. They are ready to pick when the fruit hangs downwards. All cultivated varieties are self-pollinating, so they do not need the help of the fig wasp as the wild fig does. 'Brown Turkey' – 'Fleur de Rouge' in France – is a common variety, but you could grow more authentic varieties such as the dusty carmine fig 'Rouge de Bordeaux'. 'Black Ischia' has purple skin and deep red flesh; 'White Marseilles' is very free-fruiting and has pale fruit.

oranges and lemons

Citrus fruit

Strictly speaking, citrus should not be confined to a chapter on fruits and vegetables, because one of the main reasons for growing these beautiful plants is the sublime perfume of the leaves and blossom, as well as for the loveliness of the fruit itself. (In fact, once you have the fruit hanging seductively on the bush it is extremely hard to bring yourself to pick it anyway.) Citrus fruit may have its origins in Persia, but the Mediterraneans adopted it long ago, so that the lemon, like the olive, has become an evocative symbol of the region as well as a chief industry.

Even if we cannot grow orange and lemon trees in our soil all year round, we can grow them successfully in containers, cosseting them in the finest terracotta, keeping them under glass over winter and pulling them out to enjoy the summer sun. In fact you can grow citrus fruits without a conservatory to house them; the calamondin, with its marble-sized orange fruits, is perfectly content indoors. It is always in flower or fruit. Mandarins, too, fruit well at a small size indoors. Oranges and grapefruit are less practical than lemons because the plants must be large before they will produce fruit.

Contrary to popular opinion, citrus plants are not difficult to grow, provided you do not pamper them into poor health. First, don't keep them in high temperatures all year round; they are fine in frost-free glasshouses in winter, and can even stand a touch of frost. Satsumas and kumquats are especially hardy, to −10°C/14°F. The important point is to adjust them to warmer temperatures, bringing them outdoors gradually. They will be happier

Left: *Given the conditions they enjoy, citrus fruits will grow contentedly even in fairly small pots, producing fruit from an early age.*

WHICH CITRUS TO GROW?

A good citrus nursery offers a vast choice, from 'Tahiti' limes to delicious 'Sanguinelli' blood oranges, from stripy variegated lemons to the old-fashioned Christmas tangerine, the willow-leaf mandarin. All have similar growing requirements. For a dependable lemon that flowers several times a year, choose 'Quatre Saisons'. The sour oranges deliver the best perfume: 'Bouquet de Fleurs' has lovely rounded leaves that are just as sweetly fragrant as the flowers, which are used to make oil of neroli, and the intensely scented peel of the bergamot fruit is used to make, naturally, bergamot oil. For fun, you could try a limequat, a cross between a kumquat and a lime, with bright yellow, beautifully flavoured fruits. And for authenticity grow *Citrus medica*, which bears large fruits with thick skin.

Above: *Fruit and flowers often appear on the lemon tree at the same time.*

Above: *A garden in Perugia, Italy, in which citrus fruit from an early age are massed in grand and roomy terracotta pots.*

outdoors than sweltering in a hot conservatory, so bring them out as early as possible; they will be more susceptible to pests if kept indoors.

Second, many people overwater citrus plants, which causes the fruit and leaves to drop. The secret is to water plants only when the compost (planting mix) is dry to a depth of 5cm/2in, and then water thoroughly so that it flushes right through the compost. That way, if your tap water is very hard, excess lime is flushed away too. At most, water once weekly in summer, and every three weeks in winter.

Because citrus fruits are high-performance evergreens, they need a constant, if low-level supply of nutrients, so use a specialist feed with every watering that you can also use as a regenerative spray-on foliar feed. Citrus are happiest in a soilless compost (planting mix) because it dries out more quickly than soil-based mixes.

There is no art to citrus pruning; as the plants are continuously growing, they can become quite leggy, so cut them hard back. As long as you cut above the graft union – look low down on the trunk or stem – you will not harm the plant. Better still is to keep pinching them out on a regular basis.

Above: *Many varieties of citrus fruits are cultivated in the Mediterranean, either in gardens and orchards, or else planted as street trees.*

Minimal maintenance

Imagine a glorious garden where planting

is a pleasure, not a chore, where there is

carefree

little weeding, no watering, staking or

feeding, and all that is needed is a

low maintenance

controlling hand. Welcome to the carefree

Mediterranean garden.

tough survivors

How to have healthy plants

Mediterranean plants by their nature are tough survivors, so are unlikely to come to grief as a more weakly cultivar might. And those strong – pungent, even – aromas are a real turn-off to any visiting pests. They are far more likely to turn tail and feast on your neighbour's delphiniums. *Maquis* and *garrigue* plants, with their strong scents and unpalatably thick, felty leaves, just don't appeal to your average greenfly. But in high summer, the droves of

beneficial insects – notably bees and butterflies – that crowd Mediterranean plants, especially the flowering herbs, are staggering; stop, listen and marvel at that steady buzz and drone.

Good news aside, there is no guarantee that you will not have any casualties, or be troubled by less friendly insects (though when you get bitten by mosquitoes in your back yard, you know you've got a real Mediterranean garden). Despite the leathery leaves of the agave, slugs and snails can nibble holes in them, and oleanders may be attacked by red spider mite if kept indoors for too long. Cutting them back and keeping them outdoors, sprayed regularly with water, will resolve this problem, while a sharp-edged, inhospitable gravel mulch on beds and containers should deter any but the most persistent of slugs and other slimy creatures.

CHOOSING THE BEST PLANTS

Your focus should be on growing healthy plants, which not only perform better but are more able to shrug off any potential adversaries. Make sure that the plants you bring into your garden are healthy. Buy the best specimens you can – those with promise of plentiful fresh growth – and avoid those that look spindly or have yellowing or falling leaves. Check that the plant is not root-bound – it should not have have been sitting for so long in the pot that the roots have spiralled round and round the plant – and that the roots aren't growing through the base of the pot. The plant should also be container-grown, not dug up from the ground and squeezed into the container for sale. Buying from a reputable nursery will minimize the chance of bringing vine weevil into your garden; these nasty little white grubs feed on roots and you know nothing about it until one day the plant just comes away

Left: *Mediterranean native plants, used to tough conditions, are troubled little by pest or disease.*

in your hand, leaving the other half under the soil. If you discover vine weevil in your potted plants or in your garden – the grubs are clearly visible – you can buy a water-in organic treatment consisting of tiny nematodes that will gobble up these pesky creatures.

FEEDING

Don't be tempted to "feed up" your Mediterranean plants, because rich soil, manure and fertilizer will only result in weak, sappy growth. You can, however, indulge them in the occasional seaweed spray if you want to perk up green foliage, or plants in containers. Otherwise plant them in sharply drained soil, blanket them with gravel, water them well while they establish, then leave them to sprawl and stretch out over the warm stones. Tough love, not pampering, pays off in the Mediterranean garden.

WHEN TO WATER

To put it in a nutshell: if you grow roses in a garden in the Mediterranean you'll need to water them, but if you grow Mediterranean roses – sun and rock roses – in your own garden, you won't have to. Not because it always rains in cooler climates – temperate summers are becoming hotter and drier, with weeks going by without so much as a light shower – but because Mediterranean native plants have evolved to be drought-resistant. Thus by going with nature, not fighting it, you cut out the most boring, time-consuming, gardening task – as well as any need for an irrigation system that is out of step in these times of water conservation. It might seem strange at first, but you really do not need to get out the watering can or hose to keep your drought-resistant Mediterranean native plants content.

You do need to water in a plant's first season, when it is putting down roots and establishing itself in the ground. Even the most drought-proof plant needs a good start.

Above: *English climbing roses have their place in many Mediterranean gardens, but they must be watered diligently.*

In severe summer drought, stressed plants will benefit from a water dousing. But if watering is impractical, steel yourself, and cut back plants severely so that they draw in their horns for a time. They will not look terrific at first, but they will revive in the long term.

Above: *Drought-resistant plants need watering only in their first season, until they are established.*

Above: *Golden oregano is one of many decorative herbs that need no pampering to thrive.*

Clipping and controlling

Most of the plants that make up the cultivated *maquis* do not follow the same complex rules for pruning as the majority of deciduous garden shrubs. Many *maquis* plants are aromatic evergreen shrubs or subshrubs that need pruning not so much to help them to grow full and bushy – they do that without any encouragement – but to keep them within the bounds of your garden. If the traditional gardener relies heavily on stakes, canes, string and supports to keep his herbaceous plants at their peak, your indispensable tools are your secateurs and shears, permanently sharpened.

Many of these Mediterranean plants, given the conditions they love, grow fast and need to be kept in check so that they do not grow into over-large, billowing shrubs that swamp others or steal their light. In the wild, harsh winds and grazing animals will keep many plants stunted. In your garden, given that you don't possess a herd of mountain goats, you are the controlling agent. Keep a close watch and perform surgery at a sensible time, but have one major assessment in autumn after flowering, eyeing up the different shapes and sizes, gauging the proportions.

There are few hard and fast rules here, because you might clip your thymes and rosemaries to distraction through the year anyway, using them for the cooking pot. If you do not, clipping them over after flowering will keep them in good shape and prevent them sprawling. Give thyme a radical clipping over to prevent the plant growing woody, and to promote bushiness for the next season. You might prefer your lavender leggy or clipped and compact. Either way, when you cut back the faded flower stalks, clip over the whole bush.

Above: *Clipped Mediterranean plants suit the confines of a Provençal courtyard.*

Left: *Shrubby plants such as teucrium, box and rosemary are transformed by strategic shearing.*

Regardless of season, vigorous growers such as artemesia, angelica and fennel can be hacked back when they begin to elbow neighbouring plants. Flowering shrubs such as cistus should be cut back, if they need it, after flowering, so that there is time for new buds to form. Don't leave it too late: cutting back any plant late in winter leaves it susceptible to cold weather damage because that new, fresh growth will be vulnerable.

Euphorbias should have the faded flower stalks removed, but keep your skin covered; the milky sap that drips from the stems can, and frequently does, cause nasty skin burns. You can also retard flowering by pruning at a strategic time. Santolina makes pretty lemon or yellow button-headed flowers, but often the weight of these will cause the bush to flop out from the middle. If you shear over the bush in spring, the flowers will form later than normal, and the bush will not sprawl.

Rue can be given the same delay tactics, but keep your bare skin covered, because mere contact with the silvery foliage can cause skin to become ultra-sensitive to sunlight. Oreganos will die down over winter, and the new fresh spring growth will soon cover last year's dead stalks, but you can cut these off when the new growth starts to push through. Sages can soon outgrow the area assigned to them but can be clipped back drastically in spring without suffering.

PRUNING MEDITERRANEAN SHRUBS

Some shrubby plants and herbs benefit from radical pruning to encourage fresh growth from the base, otherwise they will grow large and leggy. Another reason for radical pruning is to prevent promiscuous plants such as ballota from seeding. Plants that are frost susceptible should be cut back in spring, not autumn, which would leave new shoots vulnerable over winter.

1 △ Artemisia can be clipped to keep it within bounds at any time, but it needs radical pruning in spring.

2 △ Cut down the woody stems to 15cm/6in from the ground at a point where you can see new shoots at the base.

3 △ Go over the whole plant in the same way, cutting the stems to a uniform length and creating a rounded shape.

4 △ The trimmed shrub, invigorated by this hard pruning, will soon sprout new growth.

CREATIVE PRUNING

In spring and summer, the exuberance of the Mediterranean garden is breathtaking, but creative pruning can bring a different atmosphere to the garden later in the year. Clipping shrubs into neat, rounded shapes makes a textural tapestry of silvers, greys and greens that maintains its energy right through winter creating a quieter but equally beautiful garden.

1 △ Before you start to clip the plant, take a good look at its overall shape in the context of its neighbours and decide how you would like it to look.

2 △ As a first clip, gather up the foliage and shear around the plant.

3 △ Once you have established the right line, go over the whole plant, making a neat, rounded shape.

4 △ The final result is a satisfying, tactile cushion of foliage that works well with similarly shorn neighbours.

Propagating herbs

Because herbs are a substantial part of the Mediterranean garden, the focus here is on propagating key members of this group of plants. There are three ways of increasing your plant stock: by seed, by stem cutting and by root cuttings.

Right: *Rosemary, like other shrubby Mediterranean herbs, is simple to propagate in the autumn.*

Below: *In a Tuscan plant nursery, herbs are propagated in the cool of the early evening.*

TAKING ROOT CUTTINGS

French tarragon and mint can be propagated at any time during the growing season.

1 Fill a 2.5cm/1in cell tray with a planting mix of equal parts coir and pulverized bark, or nutrient-free soilless compost (planting mix), with a small amount of Perlite added.
2 Dig up a piece of root, and cut a short section that includes a growing node. Each growing node will produce a plant.
3 Prod each cutting into the filled tray, one per cell. Water in and label.

SOWING FROM SEED

Follow this method for spring sowing of basil, as well as thyme, oregano, sage and winter savory. All these herbs, with the exception of basil, can also be propagated by cuttings in autumn, after flowering.

If you sow seed in individual cells the seedlings tend to grow far more quickly in the limited space. They can also be coaxed out in a single block, to be potted on easily and quickly with no root disturbance. To ensure a steady intake of water for seeds, use capillary matting.

TOOLS AND MATERIALS
- cell tray with 2.5cm/1in cells
- planting mix of equal parts coir and pulverized bark, or nutrient-free soilless compost (planting mix), with a small quantity of Perlite added to keep the mix loose and free-draining
- seeds
- white paper
- Perlite
- watering can
- plant labels

1 △ Fill a cell tray with the planting mix by sweeping it across the tray. Use your thumb to make a dent in each cell to house the seed.

2 △ If you are sowing fine seeds such as oregano, fold a small piece of paper in half and pour some seed in the crease. As you tap the paper at one end, a few seeds should fall out. Aim for about ten seeds for each cell. Use the same amount for thyme and winter savory, about six per cell for basil and three for sage seed, which is larger.

3 △ Cover the cells with Perlite, previously wetted. This will reflect light and keep the seeds warm, and it does not retain water. Water the tray using a fine rose, and label. Place in a dark, warm place until the seeds germinate (about 4 – 8 days), then move them into good light and keep the compost moist.

4 △ A plug of oregano seedlings, ready to be potted on into 8cm/3¼in pot of the same compost (planting mix). If you have sown too thickly, thin them out. When seedlings develop into young, sturdy plants, harden off and plant out into the ground.

TAKING STEM CUTTINGS

Thyme, sage, winter savory and oregano can be taken from cuttings in autumn, as can rosemary, which should not be sown from seed. You can propagate the plants at the same time as you give them an autumn clipping, using the healthiest sections of the discarded soft growth.

TOOLS AND MATERIALS
- cell tray with 2.5cm/1in cells
- planting mix of equal parts coir and pulverized bark, or nutrient-free soilless compost (planting mix), with a small quantity of Perlite added
- non-flowering shoots
- secateurs (pruners)
- small flower snips
- watering can
- plant labels

1 △ Fill the cell tray with the planting mix. Using healthy, non-flowering shoots take a section above the old wood, where the fresh growth begins.

2 △ Strip off the bottom leaves, being careful not to tear the stem. With the flower snips, take a cutting just below a leaf node.

3 △ Gently push the cuttings into the tray, one per cell, but place three in a cell for thyme cuttings. Water, label and place in shade. Water regularly.

Container care

The rules change somewhat for plants that grow in containers. Because they are expected to thrive in a situation where resources are limited, these plants need a little extra attention. Watering and feeding become life essentials, although drought-resistant plants such as pelargoniums need less pampering than, say, petunias. Their other needs are free-draining compost (planting mix) and plenty of drainage material at the bottom of the pots, so that they do not sit in water.

WHEN TO WATER

The best time is in the evening, on a daily basis, when plants can take in water before much of it evaporates in the day's heat. Watering from above, with a rose fitted on the watering can, refreshes the leaves, too. If the plants look stressed during fiercely hot weather, pull them into the shade until the temperature falls.

FEEDING CONTAINER PLANTS

Plants won't die if you don't feed them, but for them to give their best, they need extra nourishment, especially after the fertilizer in the soil-based compost (soil mix) runs out after a few weeks. If you are planting a permanent evergreen, add a small handful of slow-release plant

Above: *Plant an* Arbutus unedo *in a deep pot filled with gritty compost and it will be totally content.*

fertilizer granules to the compost mix. Otherwise, during the growing season, give the plants a twice-weekly low-level liquid feed of high-potash liquid tomato fertilizer (for flowering and fruiting plants) or liquid seaweed (for foliage plants and herbs). As an occasional treat, foliar feed the leaves with a spray of dilute liquid seaweed.

LONG-TERM CARE

You cannot expect plants to keep performing when kept in the same container, year in, year out. For a couple of years, you can scrape off the top layers of compost and replace with fresh, adding a little fertilizer too. But unless you are after a bonsai effect for your Mediterranean plants you will need to re-pot, grading up a size or two. If you want to keep a container plant within bounds, always prune the roots as well as the shoots.

Left: *This terracotta pot makes an attractive container, but the danger with this design is that the curves will trap the pelargonium as the plant grows so that it cannot be removed; a pot for one season only.*

PRUNING

Plants kept permanently in pots need pruning to keep them bushy as well as to keep them small enough to be housed in a glasshouse over winter, if they are not entirely hardy. Oleanders can be cut back hard if they have grown leggy, but more usually the flowering stems should be cut back by about half, after they have flowered. Bougainvilleas benefit from pruning back after flowering if they are to maintain their prolific flower power: they can bloom three times during the summer. If you keep pelargoniums from year to year, overwintering them indoors, cut them back hard or you will never be able to move them from their conservatory shelves.

DEADHEADING

For plants such as geraniums and lantanas that flower for weeks on end, cut the faded flower stalks back to a leaf node using sharp scissors. New Guinea busy lizzies need deadheading on a daily basis to keep the flower quotient high and the faded flowers from sticking to the leaves.

HOW TO PLANT CONTAINERS

First choose your pot. An obvious statement, but the point is to make sure the container you choose will be big enough to house the plant comfortably. So, sit the plant, in its plastic pot, in the container first, remembering that you must allow for a layer of drainage at the bottom, as well as space at the top for watering.

Right: *Planted in free-draining compost, this coronilla is off to the best possible start.*

TOOLS AND MATERIALS
• stone chippings or crocks or expanded polystyrene
• container
• planting mix of three parts soil-based compost (soil mix) such as

John Innes No. 2 and one part soilless potting compost (planting mix) with a small amount of Perlite or grit
• grit, gravel or small shells
• plant label

1 ◁ Place a layer of stone chippings, crocks or expanded polystyrene in the base of the container. Broken pieces of expanded polystyrene make useful lightweight drainage material for large containers.

2 △ Cover the drainage layer with some compost and carefully tip the plant out of its plastic pot.

3 △ Settle the plant into the container, making sure there is space for watering between the soil level and the container rim. Ease planting mix around the plant, eliminating gaps but taking care not to compact the soil.

4 △ Add a layer of grit, gravel or small shells – which look pretty around the base of a large plant – to act as a water-retaining mulch and at the same time prevent the plant from becoming waterlogged. Water and label.

harsh weather

Protecting vulnerable plants in winter

One of the great bonuses of growing Mediterranean native plants is that you can have a garden full of hardy plants that are little affected by fierce weather. However, there are some borderline hardy plants that might benefit from winter protection.

Most plant losses through winter weather are from wet and wind, not frost. If you have made your plants at home in a well-drained environment, their roots will not rot and water will drain freely through the porous soil. However, rain can rot the leaves of woolly plants, such as *Salvia argentea*. For these, a simple cloche will keep the rain off. A cloche also hastens growth in spring, especially useful for bulbs. Make a simple cloche by slicing the top or bottom off a plastic drinks bottle with a knife, and pushing it into the soil around the plant. To act as a mini windbreak wall, protecting a vulnerable young plant, use the middle section only. With a bottle cloche, let in air by making holes in the bottle or leaving the top off, to prevent the plant suffering through lack of air circulation. If you use a proper cloche, prop up one side on a stone to let air in (hopefully not slugs).

Above: *For larger pots, a double layer of bubblewrap may be required to protect the plant inside from hard frost.*

Above: *Add plastic pipe lagging to vulnerable stems. Cut along the length of the lagging and wrap around.*

Above: *A cloche will protect a plant from heavy, prolonged rain.*

Wrap horticultural fleece around evergreens to protect them from scorching winds and frosts, both of which can damage leaves. The easiest way to secure the fleece around a shrub or tree is to wrap and clip it with a staple gun. Protect a young or vulnerable stem with pipe lagging.

It is easy to become neurotic and fleece everything in sight, at which point it might be easier simply to pull a duvet over the garden. But you will be surprised at how tough these plants are. The bottom section of my terraced Mediterranean garden is in a frost pocket, yet I have lost no plants to frost so far, and have protected very little.

Gravel acts as an insulator, so sometimes merely piling it up around a vulnerable plant that dies down over winter or forms a felty-leaved crown is adequate. Keeping the dead stems as a protecting cage is an extra insurance.

A last word on winter protection: if you fear that a plant has not come through, don't be too hasty in digging it up and discarding it. Some plants can turn very ragged, then make an amazing recovery when spring comes.

PROTECTING CONTAINER PLANTS IN WINTER

Plants in containers are more vulnerable than those in the ground, but much can be done to protect them. Pulling them over to the house wall is a good move; not only do they benefit from the warmth, but huddling together affords protection. If frosts threaten, you can simply throw horticultural fleece over the whole lot. Fleece kept over spring bulbs in containers will produce earlier flowers, too. Proper crocking at the base of containers, and gritty compost, will ensure that plants do not get waterlogged; the danger is not just from plants rotting, but of water freezing in the pots and making the plants freeze. Placing containers on "feet" or gravel will help water drain away. Plants in containers need little watering through winter; if they are outdoors, let the rain take care of them. Terracotta affords more protection against cold than plastic, but can still crack. Sacking or bubblewrap around the pots will protect the plant's roots as well as the container itself.

Olive trees are a perfect example of Mediterranean evergreens that will tolerate cold and frost, but not prolonged winter wet. I wrap my olive tree's container in double bubblewrap, but I don't cover the tree. If leaves are lost, fresh ones grow in spring. A cobble mulch acts as protection and a drainage medium. As a precaution, cover the stems of standard plants in pots, such as bays and rosemaries, with pipe lagging. You could cover a small bay with fleece to protect the leaves from wind damage, but you won't want to miss the first flowers on stalwart rosemary's branches.

If you don't have a conservatory, succulents will manage fine indoors. Oleanders can be completely wrapped in sacking and put to bed in a shed, or their pots wrapped and tops fleeced. Cut back bougainvilleas and pelargoniums, keeping both just ticking over on a windowsill in a light, cool room. Take cuttings of pelargoniums, not just as insurance but so you can have new plants for free every year.

Left: *Take pelargonium cuttings for the following year.*

Below: *Although most plants will come through the winter unharmed, a few will need a little bit of extra cosseting.*

A WORD ON WINDBREAKS

If your garden is exposed to harsh winds, it makes sense to protect it with windbreaks, either natural or artificial. Many of the low-growing, scrubby subshrubs have good resistance to wind, but less stalwart plants will suffer desiccated leaves and even stunted growth.

A good windbreak will protect the garden to a distance of approximately five times its height. It should filter, not block, the wind, so a woven hurdle or gappy screen is a better bet than a closely constructed fence, and an evergreen hedge is more useful than a solid wall, which creates turbulence.

Decorative living

A seat in the sun, amidst potfuls of vibrant

flowers. A wall studded with pink and red

al fresco

pelargoniums; a shell-encrusted grotto.

Here are the ideas and the inspirations that

creative containers

will enable you to create the ultimate

al fresco room.

sheltered corners

The Mediterranean courtyard

If Mediterranean *maquis* is uncontrolled and uncontrived, the Mediterranean courtyard is pure, undiluted artifice. For courtyard, read patio, terrace – windowbox, even – any place where you can display your container plants, mixing them to get high-voltage effects.

Mediterranean gardeners from Provence to Positano have a knack of displaying containers with great *élan*, whether they use them to stud a house wall, range them symmetrically on steps or bunch them closely together so that they look like an exuberant plant border. In the garden, arrange your main display around a seating area, so that the plants can be enjoyed at close quarters. The seating area should, of course, be in a nice sunny, sheltered corner to suit the plants – bougainvilleas, especially, detest windy positions. Make a display case so that the plants can all be seen clearly, and because, as in the garden proper, plants at different levels always look more interesting. Some kind of tiered shelving is ideal, or simply use piles of bricks at different levels to make plinths for the pots, arranging them so that when the containers are all in place, the supports are barely visible. Attaching metal rings to walls to hold terracotta pots is another way of bringing the eye to another level.

Below: *Make a seating area more colourful by using paints and fabrics, as well as plants.*

Above left: *Liven up dull garden railings by painting them vivid turquoise and lining up pots at their base.*

Above right: *Display plants creatively by arranging them at different levels with plinths made from bricks.*

Right: *A backdrop of sun-bleached shutters and faded wall sets the atmosphere in this courtyard garden.*

Below: *A flight of steps and a bare wall will make ideal display cases for plants.*

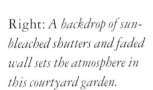

Choosing plants for your courtyard

What should you plant in pots? The brightest, boldest plants that the Mediterranean has to offer. This could include bougainvillea in all its sizzling colours, violet, cerise, flame, tangerine, which look twice as sensational grouped together. Oleanders are somewhat subtler, but stalwarts for flowering freely all through summer; particularly beautiful is the hybrid 'Soleil Levant', which really is the colour of sunrise. *Lantana camara*, which romps over wasteground in Israel, has, in the variety 'Feston Rose', luscious pink and yellow flower clusters that butterflies just cannot keep away from. You need to keep cutting off faded flowers with small, sharp scissors before the berries form, since this slows down the display. In shady corners, New Guinea busy lizzies, with practically fluorescent flowers of pink, orange and red as well as crisp white, are gloriously blatant and flower to distraction, provided you keep them well watered as they are quick to wilt in the heat. *Convolvulus sabatius*, the trailing Mediterranean bindweed, and *Anagallis monellii*, the Mediterranean pimpernel, provide the blue quotient. Potted tomatoes, aubergines (eggplants) and even firetongue beans can all be called into play to heighten the excitement level, as well as citrus trees and pomegranate bushes studded with novel, fiery orange flowers.

Include interesting silhouettes in your displays with spiky succulents such as striped *Agave americana* 'Variegata', and offset pink and red pelargoniums with the mahogany-coloured tree succulent *Aeonium arboreum*

Above: *The flower clusters of* Lantana camara, *like coloured candy, act as magnets to butterflies.*

Above: *Bougainvillea makes the biggest colour splash in courtyard or conservatory.*

Above: Anagallis monellii *has flower sprays of royal blue that will obligingly cascade from wall pots.*

Above: *Give* Nerium oleander 'Soleil Levant' *a place in the sun, and it will continue to flower profusely.*

Above: *Create an exciting display by contrasting the shapes of plants and harmonizing their colours.*

'Atropurpureum'. Dark-leaved phormiums, with their stiff, strappy leaves, are a good fan-shaped backdrop for flowers; 'Bronze Baby' is the burgundy variety that is a manageable size for containers and flatters flowers in pinks, corals and reds. Group plants together in pleasing harmonies, and use plenty of green and grey foliage to link them seamlessly.

The real beauty – and fun – of container plants is that they can be moved, and should be, as flowers, fruits and fragrances hit their peak, then fade. You just need to play scene shifter, moving the high-kickers to centre stage, relegating others to the back row of the chorus line as their moment in the spotlight passes. Have no regrets, because if you put on a good show with a strong cast, you can be sure there will be many moments in the spotlight.

Right: *For the maximum sizzle factor, team together pinks, scarlets and burgundy, then tie them all together with a rosette of striped agave.*

seashells

The charm of the grotto

Freely available from the nearest seashore, it is not surprising that seashells have always been a popular decorative medium in the Mediterranean. Even if your beachcombing is confined to the local hardware store, a prepacked bag of shells will still evoke holiday memories and a pleasurable wave of nostalgia for the seaside. Their wonderful elemental colours and textures make a perfect foil for plants, whether grouped on a garden step, encrusted on to a plain garden pot or, more adventurously, made into a garden grotto.

WALL GROTTO

This shell-encrusted wall decoration could be made smaller, larger, simpler or more ornate. I was lucky enough to have a ready-made "window" with a ledge in one garden wall, but you could adapt the same technique to make an encrusted picture for a flat wall. The technique is quite simple, but be patient; it can be fiddly and the occasional shell can slide off the wet cement. Perseverance pays off! A local seafood restaurant may be a useful source of shells, but get rid of the fishy smell by soaking them overnight in soapy water and scrubbing them thoroughly.

Above: *A shell-encrusted wall frames the green view beyond the window.*

TOOLS AND MATERIALS
• dry sand
• cement
• bucket
• water spray
• bricklayer's trowel
• rubber gloves
• an assortment of clean shells, including mussel, scallop and oyster shells
• beads (optional)

Left: *Mussel shell petals.*

Above: *The finished wall grotto, bordered with scallop shells.*

1 △ Mix together the dry sand and cement in a bucket, using four parts sand to one part cement. Add enough water to give a thick consistency. Wet the surface of the wall and apply the mortar thickly. Apply the shells to a small area at a time and keep the mortar wet.

2 △ Embed mussel shells and other small shells to make a flower; then, if you wish, add highlights by interspersing small beads around the petals.

3 △ Fill in the border of the picture with an assortment of shells, making a pleasing pattern that acts as a picture frame.

4 △ Make a simple border at the bottom of the "window" by overlapping scallop shells, inverting one at the centre for the others to flow from.

Shell pots

Like the wall grotto, these can be as simple or as elaborate as you choose. If you are just going to add a few shells as a motif, use a strong two-part resin adhesive to bond them to a terracotta pot, holding each one in place while it sets. Alternatively, you can encrust the pot completely – one advantage of total coverage is that you can conceal cracks and other imperfections.

For the best effect, use as many different varieties of small shells as you can find. Shell pots are decorative enough to display on their own, and look better with succulents or simple plants than with elaborate flowers. Grey or beige tile cement makes a neutral background, but for the dramatic black and white design featured opposite, use white tile cement.

Right: *This exquisite Moroccan design could be simplified and used to decorate a large flowerpot.*

Above: *A clutch of pots shows that even sticking on a handful of shells and beads at random has a satisfying result.*

Above: *Succulents make perfect partners for shell pots.*

TOOLS AND MATERIALS
- selection of shells
- kitchen paper
- terracotta flower pot
- tile cement
- old kitchen knife
- seed beads

Right: *Peppering this black and white shell pot with transparent seed beads gives it an icy sparkle.*

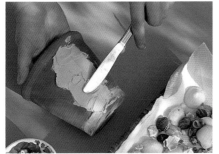

1 △ If the shells need cleaning, scrub them thoroughly and drain on kitchen paper. Clean the pot, then spread tile cement thickly over a section of the side.

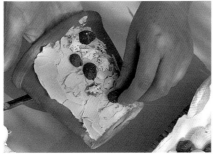

2 △ Arrange the shells in the cement, according to your own design, embedding them deeply.

3 △ If the cement is too obtrusive for your taste, sprinkle on shimmery seed beads or ground-up shells while the surface is still sticky. Shake off any excess.

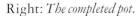

4 △ It is easier to apply the shells to the pot in sections. You can let the pot rest completely on its side as the completed section dries before starting on the next.

Right: *The completed pot.*

Evocative mosaic

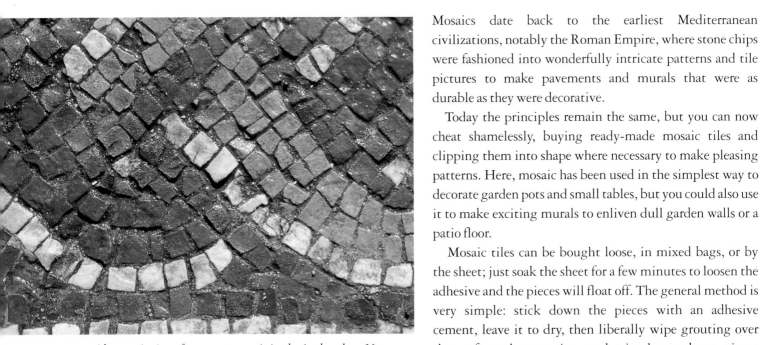

Above: *A piece of pavement mosaic in the Archaeology Museum at Sintra, Portugal.*

Mosaics date back to the earliest Mediterranean civilizations, notably the Roman Empire, where stone chips were fashioned into wonderfully intricate patterns and tile pictures to make pavements and murals that were as durable as they were decorative.

Today the principles remain the same, but you can now cheat shamelessly, buying ready-made mosaic tiles and clipping them into shape where necessary to make pleasing patterns. Here, mosaic has been used in the simplest way to decorate garden pots and small tables, but you could also use it to make exciting murals to enliven dull garden walls or a patio floor.

Mosaic tiles can be bought loose, in mixed bags, or by the sheet; just soak the sheet for a few minutes to loosen the adhesive and the pieces will float off. The general method is very simple: stick down the pieces with an adhesive cement, leave it to dry, then liberally wipe grouting over the surface; the grouting settles in the cracks to give a professional finish.

CONTEMPORARY TABLE

This garden table could not be simpler to make. Not only is the method simple, but the completely random pattern means that you do not have to consider what tile goes where. The trick is to use the same kind of mosaic tiles, which in this case are low-voltage, subtle mineral shades in ceramic that give the table a contemporary, fit-anywhere appeal. Use a small table that is portable from conservatory to terrace; you could progress next time to an outdoor dining table!

TOOLS AND MATERIALS

- small occasional table
- pencil
- ruler
- ceramic mosaic tiles
- mosaic tile adhesive
- old kitchen knife
- squeegee
- mosaic tile grouting
- damp sponge
- cloth
- scourer (Brillo)

1 △ *Draw guidelines across the centre of the table in both directions to establish the centre point. Lay the tiles, evenly spaced, along the guidelines and the table edges, buttering each tile with adhesive, using an old knife. Press into place, then fill in each quarter, keeping the spaces even.*

Above: *The natural tones of the contemporary mosaic table are complemented by the lavender.*

2 △ Using assorted colours of tiles at random makes a surprisingly pleasing pattern. If you space the tiles out evenly along the rows, you will not have to shape them to fit with nippers.

3 △ When the mosaic design is complete, leave it to dry for at least four hours. Then, using a squeegee, spread the tile grouting over the surface of the mosaic, ensuring that it fills all the cracks between the tiles.

4 △ Clean off the surplus using a damp sponge. Cover the table with a damp cloth and keep damp for two days, so that the grouting does not crack as it dries. Clean any dried grouting off the surface of the tiles using a scourer (Brillo).

shimmering tiles

Mosaic garden table and pot

BLUE MOROCCAN TABLE

The rich, saturated colours of vitreous mosaic tiles are suitable for this Moroccan-style table. To highlight the central pattern, use the occasional mirror mosaic, which reflects outdoor light beautifully. The border could be varied, and the simple repeat pattern on the centre panel extended or shortened to suit the table's dimensions. It is easy and quick to make.

Left: *The mirrored tiles sparkle in the sun.*

TOOLS AND MATERIALS
- small occasional table of metal or wood
- pencil
- ruler
- vitreous mosaic tiles
- mosaic mirror tiles
- mosaic tile adhesive
- old kitchen knife
- tile nippers
- goggles
- squeegee
- mosaic tile grouting
- cloth
- scourer (Brillo)

1 △ *Use a same-sized board or stiff paper to make a draft of the pattern for the table, drawing guidelines across the centre in both directions to establish the centre point. Lay the central pattern down first to see how it will fit on the table, and build up the boundaries on either side. When you have established the repeat pattern, replace the occasional tile with a mirror tile.*

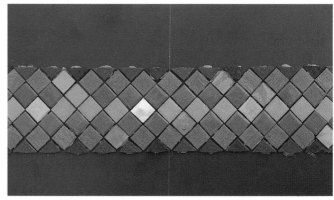

2 △ *Draw guidelines on the table in the same way, and transfer the central panel to the table, laying it from the centre point outwards, sticking each tile down as you go. To fit either end of the table, and the outer edges of the pattern, clip some tiles in half. With the nippers, grip the tile diagonally, and it should break cleanly on that line. Use goggles when cutting tiles. Then fill in.*

MOSAIC POT

The method for covering pots with mosaic is exactly the same as for the tables. Experiment with tiles left over from the larger projects. If you work on straight-sided pots, you will not need to trim the pieces of mosaic towards the base of the pot.

TOOLS AND MATERIALS
- terracotta flower pot
- mosaic tiles
- mosaic tile adhesive
- old kitchen knife
- tile nippers
- goggles
- squeegee
- mosaic tile grouting
- cloth
- scourer

Right: *Harmonizing shades are most suited to small-scale mosaics.*

△ *Clean the pot. Butter each tile with cement and apply to the side of the pot. To fit the lower rows, you will need to trim the tiles with tile nippers. Leave the adhesive to dry, then grout the mosaic.*

Right: *Use sparkling as well as matt tiles.*

splashing fountain

Water: the essential element

All gardens are the richer for some element of water, and none more so than the Mediterranean garden. Give your water feature as much space as you can, although even a trickling wall fountain placed near a seating area will prove effective, providing cool respite. If you have a pond, set it up with a submersible pump and a central or wall fountain so that the water can be circulated, making it far healthier for pond life and also adding the thrilling dimension of trickling water.

I decided to go grand for my Mediterranean garden's water feature, because, when I took on the garden, a large pond with classical proportions cried out for formal decoration. My inspiration was a ragbag drawn from the grandiose Renaissance gardens of Italy, the unparalleled water gardens of the Alhambra, and the tiled Fronteira Gardens of Portugal. This project was sheer fun and fantasy.

Left: *The Bacchus head on the new wall facade, and a plinth of bricks, await the stone shell.*

HARD LANDSCAPING

The concrete back wall was faced with limestone bricks, and a head of Bacchus in inexpensive reconstituted stone was attached. Piping was set up behind the wall to deliver water through the stone head's mouth. A simple plinth was constructed from the same materials as the wall to support a stone shell, and a channel with bricks at either side constructed beneath. The channel was lined with a heavy-duty butyl liner, concealed by large cobbles. A qualified electrician fitted the submersible pump, so that, with the flick of a switch – or a timer to control the pump – water gushes from mouth to shell, then trickles on to the cobbles beneath before meandering into the pond.

PLANTING

The bed at the back of the pond needed to be totally replanted, and as it does not get a great deal of sun, except for the far left-hand side, mostly shade-loving Mediterranean plants fill it. The back wall is covered with a mix of vines and the wonderfully named variegated ivy *Hedera helix* 'Oro di Bogliasco'. At the back of the bed is the noble Roman plant *Acanthus spinosus*, which produces large pink and brown flower spikes in late summer, and in front, *Geranium phaeum*, the mourning widow geranium.

Above: *Inspiration for the tiles was the fabulous blue-and-white* azulejos *at the Fronteira Gardens.*

By the water's edge are moisture-loving evergreen ferns *Blechnum spicant*. On the shady right-hand side, a freeform box bush hides the ugly black compartment which houses the pump mechanics, while ivies and vinca soften the hard edge of the raised bed. On the sunnier left side, the task is done with wiggly *Euphorbia myrsinites*.

DECORATING

I painted my own tiles with a simple rustic design, using special tile paints,which were then fired in the oven to set the colour. They were then applied to the wall with waterproof tile cement, and grouted afterwards. Some tiles were left off the walls to create an antique look. In Italian formal gardens pots are placed symmetrically, so identical terracotta pots of ivy-leaved *Pelargonium* 'Barbe Bleu' were added as a finishing touch with the hope that their trailing stems and rich magenta flowerheads would cascade over the edges on to the blue and white tiles, making a delicious contrast. Happily, they obliged.

Below: *The final, formal effect with newly planted backdrop, spouting Bacchus head and cascading pelargoniums.*

Above: *The pond and new wall façade before the transformation.*

Above: *Painting the tiles with a simple, strong motif that forms an effective larger pattern.*

Above: *Magenta* Pelargonium *'Barbe Bleu' complement the blue tiles.*

early flowers

The springtime container

Spring starts early in the Mediterranean garden, and even if yours is in a colder region, there are still warm, sunny days, rich with promise, that are all the more cherished for their infrequency. For those days – and even for the grey, rainy days when we gaze longingly out of the window – put on an outdoor display to gladden the eye; only fair weather gardeners, after all, reserve containers for high summer.

Easiest of all is to rank together evergreens in containers, from fan palm *Chamaerops humilis* to Roman bay. They can also serve as a green backdrop to frontline flowers. Rosemaries blossom early and together with the strokable foliage of tender lavenders – bring these in if frost is forecast – make a tactile, fragrant corner.

The heart of the display, however, is provided by vibrantly coloured Mediterranean bulbs, planted the previous autumn. Unlike chunkier hybrids, which are big and bold enough to be admired from a distance, the daintier species merit the close scrutiny that pots can provide, and are ideally suited to the confined space. Species tulips and crocuses flower gratifyingly early in the year. For the biggest golden splash, plant the golden, multi-headed Turkish native *Crocus ancyrensis* in a large pot *en masse*, or in a four-in-one container to deliver sunshine at different levels. *Tulipa linifolia* opens to a wide triangle, the petals a shimmering, bright vermilion. *Tulipa saxatilis* opens wide as a waterlily to greet the spring sun, the eggyolk yellow centres a delectable contrast to the sugar pink petals. *Tulipa clusiana* 'Cynthia' has slim flowers in soft stripes of vanilla and strawberry ice-cream. All fritillaries are delectable and most of them grow better in gravel-topped containers. And *Anemone blanda* grows beautifully in broad, shallow pans.

Left: *Pots of bulbs wait in the wings to be placed on patio or terrace.*

Opposite: *A baby* Chamaerops *palm, potted santolinas, rosemary and lavenders provide a textural evergreen display.*

Above: Crocus minimus *(left) has feathery markings, while* Crocus etruscus *(right)supplies the softest shade of lavender.*

Left: *Dainty* Tulipa clusiana *'Cynthia' grows well in pots and has the prettiest stripy blooms.*

Caerulean blue

Pots of grape hyacinths

Create a cascade of richest blue by planting several different varieties of grape hyacinth in each pot and lining the garden steps with them, or cluster the pots together to make a textural blue carpet to brighten the earliest weeks of the year. You could follow the same simple method of bulb planting and create a similar effect with different kinds of crocus in shades of yellow or mauve.

TOOLS AND MATERIALS
• terracotta pots
• stone chippings
• soil-based compost (soil mix) such as John Innes No. 2
• *Muscari latifolium* (two-tone, ink and powder blue)
• *Muscari armeniacum* (conical, bright blue)
• *Muscari comosum* (tassel-headed)
• pale grit or gravel

1 ◁ Line the base of the pot with stone chippings for drainage.

2 △ Half-fill the pot with soil-based compost (soil mix) and place the bulbs, equally spaced, across the surface of the compost. Use seven bulbs for a 12cm/4¾in pot; nine bulbs for a 15cm/6in pot.

3 △ Fill to 2cm/¾in from the top with compost.

4 △ Top with a layer of pale grit or gravel.

Above and left: *Grape hyacinths, all the same or in different varieties, make a striking display for early spring.*

Below: *Grown in gravel-topped terracotta pots,* Anemone blanda *produces foliage first, flowers second.*

effortless style

Pelargonium power

It isn't hard to name the number one Mediterranean container plant, a colourful descendant of the prolific South African wildflower of the same name. The pelargonium, or bedding geranium, is everywhere in the Mediterranean, pinned haphazardly to the humblest house wall and gracing the grandest palazzo terrace; equally at home in tin oil can or terracotta oil jar. Pots of zonal bedding geraniums in the zingiest reds and pinks are just as popular as the ivy-leaved and smaller balcony varieties, which cascade effortlessly from windowboxes at all heights. Even those that are neglected carry on flowering for months. But for the most magnificent display, feed your pelargoniums twice weekly with liquid tomato fertilizer, water them regularly – though they need less water than most bedding plants – and encourage future flowers by cutting spent stems right back to the leaf joint they grew from.

Above: *Planted in pots and ranged at intervals, trailing pelargoniums tumble beguilingly over a stone wall.*

Left: *Brighten a bare wall with pots of pelargoniums, slotted into metals rings to fit the rims of the terracotta pots.*

Right: *Two familiar sights in southern Italy: the Vespa motorcycle and pelargoniums decorating a house wall.*

Above: *Sugar-pink ivy-leaved pelargoniums show their climbing capabilities by reaching the roof of this garden outhouse.*

Left: *Steps, railings and walls all present potential display cases for pelargoniums.*

TAKING CUTTINGS

If you cannot provide pelargoniums with frost-free conditions over winter, consign them to the compost heap, but take cuttings in late summer to produce next year's plants. Use non-flowering shoots and cut cleanly just below a leaf joint. Push gently into free-draining soilless compost (planting mix), several cuttings to a pot, and keep moist on a cool, sunny windowsill.

Below: *Double-flowered pelargonium.*

The ornamental pot

There can be no material more sympathetic to plants than the ground from which they spring, which is why baked earth – in Latin, *terra cotta* – cannot be bettered as a container choice. There is not a flower or foliage plant that is not enhanced by its natural elegance. Terracotta can be charmingly rustic, plain and simple, or gloriously Renaissance, swagged and garlanded. The warm tones of terracotta flatter the plant, and its porous quality allows the plant to "breathe" so that the roots are kept comfortingly cool. Regretfully, plastic imitations never match up to the real thing, and it is worth paying that little bit extra for a hand-made pot, because it will have its own distinctive imperfections to add to its appeal.

Give pots a weathered appearance by painting on milk, yogurt or diluted cow manure to encourage algae and lichens. And, even if you have to hold it together with a girdle of wire, never, ever throw away an antique terracotta pot. Keep a permanent eye out for unusual, decorative containers old and new, because the pot can be every bit as important as the plant.

Above: *On a whitewashed roof in Greece, a pot in clear tones of bright blue and yellow contrasts with a scarlet pelargonium.*

Above: Echeveria *make the ideal swirly topping for an antique terracotta urn, corseted with heavy wire to keep it from collapsing.*

Right: *Sometimes, as in the case of this baroque terracotta container, the pot becomes more important than the plants within it.*

Left: *The Mediterranean region offers a wealth of decorative painted pots.*

Painted pots

The uniformity of machine-made terracotta pots lends them to decorating, and they are inexpensive enough to experiment with. Simplest is to give them a lick of paint, which will not last for ever, but once you start wielding the paintbrush you will want to change them seasonally, anyway. Alternatively, use this simple technique to emulate the fancy colour-marbled pots of Majorca.

TOOLS AND MATERIALS
- broad paintbrush
- matt emulsion (latex) paint
- terracotta pots
- wire
- rubber gloves
- plastic washing-up bowl
- stick
- gloss paint in darker, contrasting shade

1 ◁ Terracotta pots can be dipped for marbling without first being painted, but a contrast base colour makes a more dramatic effect. For the marbled effect, make a wire handle for a painted pot by running a length of wire through the hole in the base to form a circle, and twisting at the top to secure. Fill a plastic bowl with water. Dip a stick into stirred gloss paint and drizzle on to the surface of the water, swirling the paint into patterns.

2 ▷ Using the wire handle, dip the painted pot into the water so that gloss paint adheres to one side of the pot.

3 ◁ Turn the pot over carefully and dip the other half into the water.

4 ▷ Hang up the pot, still on its wire handle, and leave to dry for 24 hours. The pot in the foreground (right) has been painted yellow and dipped in blue.

Above: *Apply one or two coats of emulsion (latex) paint to each pot, allowing time to dry between coats.*

Above: *A few strokes of turquoise matt emulsion paint transforms these plain machine-made terracotta pots.*

Above: *These pots are about to have the marbled treatment, but look pretty just as they are, painted pink and lemon.*

Above: *Clever use of colour improves not just the pot, but the plinth it is standing on.*

Left: *The matt pink and lemon pots, marbled with contrasting gloss paint.*

Plant directory

Mediterranean plants are an intoxicating

mixture of scrubland vagrants and

shrubs and trees

glamorous hybrids, wayside weeds and

exotic immigrants. Make your personal

perennials

selection to create the headiest combination

of all in your own garden.

plant directory

Shrubs and subshrubs

PLANT DIRECTORY NOTES
- This list is by no means exhaustive, but it represents those plants most suited to Mediterranean garden cultivation.
- Unless otherwise stated, all the plants prefer a sunny outlook and well-drained soil.

KEY TO SYMBOLS
FT Plant may be damaged by temperatures below 5°C/41°F
*   Half hardy: plant can withstand temperatures down to 0°C/32°F
** Frost hardy: plant can withstand temperatures down to –5°C/23°F
*** Fully hardy: plant can withstand temperatures down to –15°C/5°F

Evergreen shrubs and subshrubs – plants that are woody only at the base – form the backbone of the Mediterranean landscape. Some are also aromatic herbs. For thyme, rosemary, sage, oregano and winter savory, see pages 86–7.

ARTEMISIA ***

Pale silvery green, fine, ferny foliage and a strong aroma make southernwood (*Artemisia abrotanum*) distinctive; in summer, it produces dense yellow flowerheads, and reaches a height of 1m/39in.

Absinthe was made from *Artemisia absinthium*, which is one of the bitterest herbs known. The grey foliage is finely divided and, in summer, sprays of small, yellow flowers appear. Grows to 1m/39in, with a larger spread. The smaller *absinthium* cultivar 'Lambrook Silver' has finely cut silvery leaves and sprays of yellow bobble flowers.

BALLOTA PSEUDODICTAMNUS **

Horehound grows wild on rocky Cretan hillsides and has naturalized in Italy. It is also grown in gardens for its wonderfully woolly foliage. The lemon green stems have rounded leaves, and, in summer, whorls of seed vessels, which are more ornamental than the small lilac flowers. *Ballota* regenerates from the base like a perennial, but needs protection from prolonged wet. It grows to 60cm/24in, with a larger spread.

BOUGAINVILLEA FT

No Mediterranean garden is complete without a small flourish – or extravagant cascade – of sumptuous, vibrantly coloured bougainvillea. It is the bracts, not the unnoticeable flowers, that produce the show. Unless you live in a Mediterranean region, be content with growing bougainvillea in a large container in a sheltered, sunny spot, where it should flower several times in one season. Regular light pruning, especially after flowering, will keep the plant in good shape. Feed it with general liquid fertilizer such as seaweed at the start of the growing season and coax it into flower with liquid tomato feed. Overwinter under glass.

BUPLEURUM FRUTICOSUM **

A graceful, aromatic *garrigue* evergreen, bupleurum provides attractive deep green, leathery leaves and dainty yellow flower sprays on upright stems. Usefully, it grows in shade, and is good as a filler plant. It can reach 2.5m/8ft, but is easy to clip back.

BUXUS see pages 56–7.

CISTUS **

Evergreen and evergrey aromatics of *garrigue* and *maquis*, the rock rose family supplies possibly the most ornamental of all the Mediterranean flowers. The crumpled, five-petalled papery blooms, in shades from cerise to pure white, open with the sun and soon fall, making a progression of flowers through early summer. Some varieties, such as the gum cistus, *C. ladanifer*, have sticky foliage which yields ladanum, a resinous substance the ancient Greeks burnt for its scent; it is still used in the perfume industry.

There are many species and hybrids of cistus, but all need protection from cold winds and heavy frost; prune out any frost-damaged stems in spring. Taking cuttings in summer is an insurance.

C. incanus ssp. *creticus* has crinkly oval leaves, hairy stems and flamboyant deep pink flowers with orange stamens. It grows up to 1m/39in. *C. parviflorus* is similar, but the flowers are smaller and a soft pink.

C. ladanifer may reach 2.5m/8ft. It has distinctive deep green lance-shaped leaves. The large white flowers, which grow up to 10cm/4in across, occasionally have a ring of five deep plum blotches around the golden stamens.

The narrow-leaved cistus, *C. monspeliensis*, is a compact, many-branched shrub with small white flowers that grows in large groups in the *maquis;* it looks good grouped in gardens, too, growing up to 1m/39in.

C. x *purpureus* is one of the showiest rock roses, with large deep rose flowers with plum-blotched centres. It can reach a height of 120cm/48in.

Artemisia *'Lambrook Silver'*.

Bougainvillea.

Bupleurum fruticosum.

Cistus ladanifer.

Cistus *'Sunset'*.

Convolvulus cneorum.

Coronilla glauca.

Euphorbia wulfenii.

C. x *pulverulentus* 'Sunset', a sprawling hybrid (up to 75cm/30in) with rich cerise flowers, is garden-worthy because it blooms for weeks until the end of summer.

CONVOLVULUS CNEORUM **

The sheeniest of silver shrubs grows on rocks by the sea and catches the light like no other; in sunshine, the small, silky leaves look as if they could be made of fine metal sheeting. Rose-tinted buds open wide in early summer to fluted white trumpet flowers with yellow centres. It will reach about 50cm/20in.

CORONILLA VALENTINA ssp. GLAUCA **

Given a warm, sheltered site, this clifftop shrub produces bright yellow pea-like flowers smelling of ripe peaches for months, hitting its peak in spring. The leaves are pretty too, held on stiff stems in dainty sprays. It makes an ideal wall shrub. The cultivar 'Citrina' has lemon flowers. Cut it back after flowering to prevent ungainly growth.

EUPHORBIA

This is an important family of garden-worthy plants that were valued in ancient Greece for their purgative properties. Gardeners would do better to be wary of the milky sap that can give skin nasty burns: always wear gloves when pruning euphorbias. Greece alone has 43 species of spurge, but the best known – and most valued – to gardeners is *Euphorbia characias***, which grows in the western Mediterranean,

and makes a handsome clump of variably blue green or grey green foliage. In spring the stiff stems carry great heads of lime green flowers, each centred with a red nectar gland, that look rather like frogspawn. *E. characias* ssp. *wulfenii*, which grows in the eastern Mediterranean, is similar but larger, reaching up to 150cm/5ft, and has no red centre to the flower.

*Euphorbia myrsinites**** is absolutely essential in the Mediterranean garden. It is a low-growing sprawler, with wonderful, wiggly, grey blue shoots, densely packed with   blue green pointed leaves; in spring, they produce the typical lime green froth of spurge flowers.

GENISTA ***

The tough, drought-proof gorses are invaluable in the Mediterranean garden for their mass of golden flowers as much as their resilience. Two of the best are *Genista lydia*, which has a stiff network of spiny leaves on woody stems, and larger *Genista hispanica*, Spanish gorse, which has the prickliest thorns; 75cm/30in tall, it has a spread of 150cm/5ft. Both are good planted on the edge of a raised bed to cascade over the edge, and both flower voraciously in spring.

HALIMIUM LASIANTHUM **

One of the rock rose family, this native of Spain and Portugal has rich yellow flowers which sometimes have a deep red blotch at the base of each petal. It can reach a height of 1m/39in with a spread of 150cm/5ft.

x HALIMIOCISTUS WINTONENSIS **

This enchanting rock rose hybrid has beautiful markings on saucer-shaped white flowers of deep crimson bands around the golden stamens. Up to 60cm/24in, it has a wider spread.

HELIANTHEMUM NUMMULARIUM ***

The rock or sun roses, close relations of cistus, create carpets of colour that spread over stones, sprawl across paths or smother low walls from early summer onwards. The species has yellow or orange flowers, but there are masses of named varieties to choose from with a wide variety of flower colour and with foliage varying from pale grey to deep green.

Bright orange 'Henfield Brilliant', grey-leaved 'Wisley Primrose' and 'Wisley White' are just three that are ideally suited to the Mediterranean garden. Cut back flowered stems to prevent straggling plants.

HELICHRYSUM ITALICUM **

Fine, silvery foliage is the main attribute of the curry plant, which smells somewhat incongruous in the Mediterranean garden, but contributes to the spicy *maquis* aroma. In midsummer, lemon yellow flowerheads are produced. It grows to 60cm/24in. Shorter and neater at 20cm/8in, *Helichyrsum italicum* ssp. *microphyllum* has stiff stems and the squiggliest silver foliage.

HELLEBORUS ARGUTIFOLIUS see
pages 56–7.

Genista lydia.

x Halimiocistus wintonensis.

H. *'Henfield Brilliant'*.

H. i. *ssp.* microphyllum.

Hyssopus officinalis.

Lantana camara.

Lotus hirsutus.

Myrtus communis.

HYSSOPUS OFFICINALIS ***

This aromatic bush with narrow, dark green leaves has generous spikes of deep blue flowers in midsummer. Its height is 80cm/32in, its spread wider. *H. o. albus* has white flowers. Dead-head after flowering and trim the plant in spring to keep it tidy. Rock hyssop, *H. officinalis* ssp. *aristatus*, is similar but smaller, reaching only 30cm/12in.

LAMPRANTHUS see pages 66–7.

LANTANA CAMARA FT

The prettiest flowerheads of flame and yellow, or pink and lemon, depending on the cultivar, compensate for *Lantana*'s prickly leaves and unpleasant smell. *Lantana* makes the perfect summer container plant, provided you trim faded flowers and berries as they form. Bring it in for winter.

LAURUS NOBILIS **

The bay tree's height and spread can reach 10m/33ft in the wild; in cultivation it is often grown as a clipped standard. It has yellow green flower clusters and black berries, but the handsome leaves are the main feature.

LAVANDULA see pages 64–5.

LOTUS HIRSUTUS **

A small *maquis* and *garrigue* gem, growing to 60cm/24in, with woolly, palest grey foliage. The rose-white pea flowers in summer are followed by clusters of dark red shiny seed pods. Clip it back in spring.

MYRTUS COMMUNIS **

A symbol of love and beauty since ancient times, with aromatic bark, leaves and flowers, myrtle grows in the *maquis*, by streams and on scrub. Small, dark green glossy leaves and white flower clusters in spring, followed by small dark purple berries, make it a covetable garden plant.

Unless you can provide *Myrtus communis* with a warm wall or sheltered site, where it can grow up to 3m/10ft tall, plant it in a large container. Sardinians make an oil from myrtle berries that they claim is superior to olive oil. Another wonderful variety, tarentine myrtle or *Myrtus communis* ssp. *tarentina*, grows mainly by the coast (see pages 66–7).

NERIUM OLEANDER FT

Like bougainvillea, oleander is frequently planted on walkways, parks and gardens throughout the Mediterranean, but it is also widely naturalized. Given a warm, sunny spot, oleanders flower right through summer, and make superb, surprisingly tough, container plants. They may survive several degrees of frost, but protect over winter if you are in a frost-prone area.

They are inclined to grow large and leggy, but they can be cut back hard to encourage new growth; however, be prepared to lose the following summer's blooms. Spray the whole plant frequently with water to discourage their big enemy, sap-sucking red spider mite. All parts of the plant are extremely poisonous.

PHILLYREA ***

Phillyrea angustifolia is a member of the olive family, evergreen with lance-shaped leaves of rich green that grow on upright branches. Small, greenish yellow, fragrant flowers are followed by pea-sized, deep blue fruit. It will reach 2.5m/8ft, and makes a handsome container plant. *Phillyrea latifolia* is a taller shrub or tree with leaves that are oval on the young plant, lance-shaped when mature. It is suited to part shade.

PHLOMIS **

Jerusalem sage, *Phlomis fruticosa*, grows wild on dry, rocky hillsides. It makes an evergreen bush about 150cm/5ft high, with pale green felty foliage and stems, along which large hooded flowers of rich yellow are carried in dense whorls. Once they have flowered, the dead heads persist on the stems, and look like circular pale green honeycombs.

From the Balearics, *Phlomis italica* is just 30cm/12in high, with a wider spread, and it has the delectable combination of pale grey green woolly foliage and ice pink flowers.

PITTOSPORUM TOBIRA **

A native of China and Japan, *Pittosporum tobira* is widely grown in parks and gardens in the Mediterranean, sometimes as a hedge. Large rosettes of long, oval, shiny leaves and sublimely fragrant white waxy flowers make this lush evergreen rather glamorous. It can reach 5m/16ft. It grows well in a container, which is an advantage if you cannot offer it a sunny, sheltered spot.

Nerium oleander.

Phillyrea angustifolia.

Phlomis fruticosa.

Pittosporum tobira.

Prunus lusitanica.

Rosa pimpinellifolia.

Ruta graveolens.

Santolina ch. 'Lemon Queen'.

PRUNUS LUSITANICA **

A dense evergreen native of rocky habitats, the Portugal laurel makes a fine clipped tree, but can grow to 20m/65ft if neglected. In summer, the tassel-like white flowers appear in profusion, and they are followed by oval purplish black fruits. Suited to part shade.

ROSA ***

Though roses are widely cultivated in gardens throughout the Mediterranean, the true native rose is probably the cistus, or rock rose (see pages 146–7). But as the origin of the gallica rose is thought to be Damascus, it seems appropriate to include *Rosa gallica* var. *officinalis*. Rich pink flowers smother the 150cm/5ft bush of dense foliage in early summer, and have golden stamens and an exceptional fragrance.

There are two wild roses you could also consider: *Rosa pimpinellifolia*, the burnet rose, which has white flowers and black hips (1m/39in) and *Rosa pendulina*, the small, pretty Alpine rose with pendulous branches, greyish green foliage and single deep pink flowers followed by urn-shaped hips.

RUTA GRAVEOLENS ***

Rue is a 60cm/24in evergreen shrub with glaucous blue fern-like foliage. In summer, it produces small sprays of yellow flowers. *R. g.* 'Jackman's Blue' has the bluest foliage. Shape the bush in spring, and cut back after flowering in summer, but beware of handling the plant in full sun or after rain as it can cause a severe skin reaction.

SALVIA OFFICINALIS 'PURPURASCENS' ***

The purple-leaved form of sage makes a perfect foil for all those grey and silver shrubs such as helichrysum, santolina, lavender and rue. Focus on the foliage, not the flowers, by clipping it back in spring to encourage fresh new leaves. Plant small, and cut back.

SANTOLINA **

Cotton lavender, *Santolina chamaecyparissus*, is neither lavender nor cotton, but is a member of the daisy family; a clue to this are the button-like yellow flowerheads held above the silver aromatic foliage, which has the appearance of fine coral. It grows to 75cm/30in with a spread of 1m/39in. *Santolina rosmarinifolia* has bright green foliage similar to rosemary; *S. pinnata* ssp. *neapolitana* has feathery green foliage and creamy button flowers. Different santolinas look good planted in a group, clipped into tactile cushions.

SPARTIUM JUNCEUM **

Spanish broom lines many roads in the South of France, and in early summer fills the air with its gorgeous honey-vanilla scent. The flexible, rush-like green stems, used in ancient Greece for making the sails of ships, and still used today for basket-weaving, produce masses of large, bright yellow pea-like flowers, which are followed by flat green seed pods.

Grow *Spartium junceum* from seed because it does not like being transplanted, and, besides, it grows fast. If you are saving seed, sow it straight away or keep it in the pods until spring. Spanish broom can reach 3m/10ft in height and spread, but it is best kept compact by careful spring pruning; don't cut beyond green wood.

TEUCRIUM FRUTICANS **

The tree germander of *garrigue* and *maquis* is a sprawling evergreen shrub of silvery grey leaves and stems with soft lavender blue flowers that bloom from early spring for several months. It can grow to 2.5m/8ft tall, but it is easily cut back, and best grown against a wall.

VIBURNUM TINUS ***

The workhorse shrub of gardens originates in Mediterranean scrub and open woodland, where it can grow to 7m/23ft. Laurustinus has oval, leathery evergreen leaves and rosy white dense flowerheads in spring and summer, which are followed by clusters of dark blue, poisonous berries that have a metallic sheen.

YUCCA

This showy American shrub is widely cultivated in the Mediterranean and has occasionally naturalized. Sword-like leaves make a stiff basal rosette from which springs the spectacular flower stalk, dripping with creamy white pendulous flowers in summer. The leaves of *Yucca gloriosa*** are frighteningly sharp; *Yucca filamentosa*** has twisted threads along the edges of its foliage. Grow yucca only if you can give it space.

Spartium junceum.

Teucrium fruticans.

Viburnum tinus.

Yucca gloriosa.

Perennials

These are just some of the perennials that grow wild in the Mediterranean and will translate well to the cultivated garden. Plant them, if possible, in generous drifts to flow in and around shrubs. As they mature, they will soon fill your garden.

ACANTHUS see pages 56–7.

ANTHEMIS TINCTORIA ***
A wasteland weed that was once used to make a good yellow dye, the yellow chamomile makes a good garden plant, especially if you cheat and use a cultivar such as the prolific lemon-headed 'E. C. Buxton'. The foliage makes a mound of pretty, ferny green leaves in summer, and the straight stems reach about 50cm/20in.

ARMERIA see pages 66–7.

CATANANCHE CAERULEA ***
A plant of dry grassland, pretty *Catananche* has grey-green grassy leaves and papery, violet-centred lavender ruffled flowers with translucent bracts at the base, held on wiry stems up to 50cm/20in high. It flowers for weeks over the summer and can be sown from seed in spring.

CENTRANTHUS RUBER ***
The valerian that grows in rocky places in the Mediterranean will also self-seed in nooks and crannies of garden walls, as well as in gravel. Spires of red, pink or white, scented funnel flowers appear in spring and summer; the grey green foliage is almost waxy. It prefers an alkaline soil.

CONVOLVULUS
Convolvulus althaeoides *** is the best kind of bindweed. Plant it at the base of purple sage, where the fine, silvery stems, about 60cm/24in long, will twist and twine in and around the dark leaves, throwing out ice pink trumpet flowers that make a great contrast, but be careful: the roots spread as fast as the stems. It is ideal for a container.

Convolvulus sabatius ** is another luscious bindweed that, given plenty of sun, produces endless powder blue trumpet flowers from midsummer; a darker form with rich royal blue flowers is a little less free-flowering. Its wonderful tumbling habit is suited to raised beds, terraces and containers. Although the top growth may be killed by frosts, the plant re-shoots from the base the following year.

*DIANTHUS****
The daintiest species pinks grow in rocky habitats around the Mediterranean, notably the rich pink *Dianthus haematocalyx*. The garden cultivars are more readily available, and are ideal for well-drained stony soil.

DIGITALIS ***
Mediterranean foxgloves have a subtle charm. *Digitalis parviflora* grows in the mountains of Spain; it will grow in sun or shade, and has tightly packed 60cm/24in spires of chocolate-shaded flowers. *D. ferruginea*, a self-seeding biennial, is a taller, larger species reaching 90cm/36in, with stems of honey rust trumpet flowers. It grows in woody habitats and is quite at home in light shade. *D. viridiflora* offers novel flower spikes of yellow green. Foxgloves are summer flowering.

Anthemis t. *'E. C. Buxton'*.

Catananche caerulea.

Centranthus ruber.

Echium pininana.

Convolvulus sabatius.

Dianthus *cultivar*.

Digitalis ferruginea.

ECHINOPS RITRO***

The glamorous globe thistle of Mediterranean mountain pastures produces steel blue, fuzzy flowerheads in late summer, which are a magnet to bees and butterflies. Cut back the spiny, silvery green foliage if it gets ragged, but leave the dried heads on their 120cm/48in stems to decorate the garden in autumn.

ECHIUM FT

Echium candicans, the Pride of Madeira is, alas, not the pride of the Mediterranean, but as it flourishes in its gardens and is such a sensational plant, it deserves a mention. In summer, showcase spires of 1–2m/3–6ft, thickly studded with blue and mauve flowers, shoot from grey green rosettes of pointed leaves; like its humbler relative *Echium vulgare*, it is a great attracter of bees. It is easy to sow from seed, though hard to hang on to in any but warm, frost-free sites, and is short-lived at any rate. It is a close relative of the larger *Echium pininana*, which is hardier, but grows to an unwieldy, sensational 3.5m/12ft. If you have the space, plant 150cm/5ft apart, and stand well clear.

ERYNGIUM ***

The roots of the sea holly were used medicinally in ancient Greece to reduce swellings. Modern gardeners prefer to grow them as highly ornamental plants, distinguished by their striking metallic foliage and thistle flowers collared with spiky, sometimes feathery, bracts.

Mediterranean shores boast over ten species, of which *Eryngium maritimum* (see pages 66–7) and late-flowering, deep blue *E. amethystinum*, 45cm/18in, are the best. Their Iranian relative *E. giganteum*, 90cm/36in, is impressive and does not look out of place. Also worth growing are *E. alpinum*, *E. bourgatii* and *E.* ✕ *zabelii*.

GERANIUM ***

The tuberous cranesbill of southern Spain, *Geranium malviflorum*, produces, in spring, the prettiest soft mauve flowers in branched clusters, and handsomely cut leaves. In summer the plant is dormant, but it springs up again amazingly in autumn, reaching 30cm/12in high, with an even wider spread.

Geranium tuberosum is similar to *G. malviflorum*, but has smaller, pink flowers and the foliage is more finely cut. It grows up to 20cm/8in high.

LINARIA PURPUREA ***

A native of southern Italy and Sicily, purple toadflax makes tall, slim spires of deep mauve flowers, which always seem to self-seed in the tiniest nooks and crannies.

LINUM NARBONENSE ***

The daintiest azure blue or violet flax of the western Mediterranean grows in open, rocky habitats, and needs the same situation in the garden to show it to its best advantage. Linum is easy to sow from seed in spring and then plant out in summer.

SALVIA ***

Salvia argentea is one of the showiest sages. In spring, a rosette of large silvery-white leaves appears; covered in fine down, the foliage feels like the silkiest fur. In summer, the down disappears; but in spring, 60cm/24in stems of tiered white flowers appear, like chandeliers.

It is surprising that *Salvia sclarea*, an unpleasantly scented plant of scrub and roadsides, is used in perfumery, but the clary sage has other merits: handsome, heart-shaped leaves and stiff stems laden with sage flowers of diaphanous white and lilac. It reaches 1m/39in high and 30cm/12in wide, and it is perennial or biennial. *Salvia sclarea* var. *turkestanica* has pink stems of rose-tinged white flowers.

SILYBUM MARIANUM ***

The milk thistle of olive groves and open woodland is widely grown in Mediterranean gardens because the veined, green foliage is so striking; in summer, purple flowerheads appear on stems of 150cm/5ft high.

STACHYS BYZANTINA ***

Woundwort, which has naturalized in the Mediterranean, supplies mat-forming, palest grey foliage, which meanders around other plants, hiding ugly bases and providing flattering contrast. In summer, equally woolly stems of whorled, palest pink flowers appear on stems of 45cm/18in. 'Silver Carpet' is a useful non-flowering cultivar, with a focus on intensely silver foliage.

Eryngium giganteum.

Linum narbonense.

Silybum marianum.

Geranium malviflorum.

Linaria purpurea.

Salvia argentea.

Stachys byzantina.

plant directory

Annuals and biennials

These plants you can sow easily from seed. Although they will not be permanent inhabitants of your Mediterranean garden, they all share the great virtue of filling spaces temporarily with pools of vivid colour.

CALENDULA OFFICINALIS ***
The hardy annual pot marigold has naturalized throughout the Mediterranean, and although it may not have done so in the *maquis*, it looks wonderful contrasting with silver and grey shrubs. Sow seed in spring.

CERINTHE MAJOR 'PURPURASCENS' *
This extraordinary form of the annual wayside honeywort forms a chunky clump of glaucous blue leafy stems about 45cm/18in high, topped with purple and sea blue tubular bracts that hold clusters of dusky maroon nodding flowers. It flowers from late spring through summer, and self-seeds prolifically in gravel. Sow in spring and plant out when there is no further risk of frost.

ECHIUM VULGARE ***
Bristly biennial viper's bugloss grows in fields and olive groves. It is worth growing in the Mediterranean garden for the striking blue, pink and purple flowers that are borne on one or several stems.

GALACTITES TOMENTOSA ***
A wasteland thistle that is also an elegant, self-seeding garden annual. The serrated foliage is veined in silver, and the basal rosette makes a striking pattern on gravel. In summer, dainty, fluffy pink flowers appear on 60cm/2ft stems.

HELIANTHUS ANNUUS ***
Spanish explorers bought the sunflower to Europe from the Americas in the 16th century, although it is hard to imagine a time when Provence had no sunflower fields. Many hybrids exist in shades ranging from white to deep burgundy, and dwarf varieties have been introduced for gardeners who like their flowers neat and tidy. But for a real splash of Provençal sunshine, grow the classic, tall, annual, yellow sunflowers with dinner plate faces and watch the ramrod stems soar above your head, provided you feed and water them. Sow seed in spring into the ground or pots, and don't grow them in the same spot twice.

This is one flower that does not belong in the simulated *maquis*, but it looks wonderful in a row, to mark a boundary or hide an ugly background.

IPOMOEA PURPUREA see pages 62–3.

LATHYRUS see pages 62–3.

LUPINUS VARIUS *
If you are lucky enough to obtain seed of this annual brilliant blue lupin, which frequents sandy ground, sow it in the ground in spring, in a sunny, sheltered area. It grows to 60cm/24in or more.

Calendula officinalis.

Galactites tomentosa.

Cerinthe major *'Purpurascens'*.

Echium vulgare.

Helianthus annuus.

Lupinus varius.

Papaver carmeli.

Papaver somniferum.

Verbascum thapsus.

PAPAVER ***

Papaver carmeli is the rich red annual poppy of northern Israel that grows up to 60cm/24in high; if you are lucky enough to get hold of some seed, sow direct in spring, thinning out the seedlings. Two other more common poppies that frequent waysides and waste places throughout the Mediterranean are the opium poppy *Papaver somniferum*, with the familiar lilac flowers and blue grey foliage, and the common scarlet field poppy *Papaver rhoeas.*

TOLPIS BARBATA ***

Dark-centred deep lemon daisies on stems up to 60cm/24in spring from a green rosette of foliage. Sow in late summer and the long tap root will establish, so that it can plumb the ground the following summer to find moisture, as it does in the *garrigue*. It will also do well as a spring-sown hardy annual. If you want a cut flower from your Mediterranean garden, this should be your first choice.

VERBASCUM ***

Many mulleins grow wild in the Mediterranean. One of the most impressive is the woolly, near white biennial, *Verbascum thapsus*, which has a statuesque spike of yellow flowers that grows from an impressive basal rosette. It looks good as a feature plant, surrounded by gravel, and can reach 2m/6ft. Made to feel at home, it will produce more plants for the following year. *Verbascum chaixii* reaches a more modest 150cm/5ft, and has branching stems packed with purple-eyed white or yellow flowers.

Grasses

Decorative grasses, with their vertical form and feathery textures, add a unique quality to the Mediterranean garden. Plant them in isolation so that their breezy style is not cramped.

BRIZA MAXIMA ***

Nodding, purplish green flowerheads rather like scaly fish tremble in the breeze, and make the annual large quaking grass a novel feature. In late summer, the plant is an attractive golden straw shade, and is much used in decorative dried flower arrangements; it reaches 60cm/24in. Common quaking grass, *Briza media*, is a similar perennial species that can reach 90cm/36in.

STIPA ***

There are two chief stipa grasses of the Mediterranean: needle grass, *Stipa pennata*, which has long, fine, feathery wisps to its thin leaves, 30cm/12in high, and *Stipa tenacissima*, esparto grass, which is much more robust and reaches150cm/5ft. *Stipa tenuifolia* is more readily available as a garden plant, and it supplies a stunning effect when it flowers in summer, the thick silken fringe of corn blonde swaying sensuously in the wind at a height of 90cm/36in. All are perennial.

Briza maxima.

Stipa tenuifolia

plant directory

Trees

Most trees in the Mediterranean region are evergreen, and, although you may not be able to grow a full scale pine tree that is typical of the region, there are plenty of attractive options that you can grow either in the ground or in containers. Just one palm tree, even if you grow it in a pot, will add tremendous atmosphere to the garden, as well as making a strong architectural feature. If feasible, spray the leaves regularly.

ACACIA
Mimosas and acacias, introduced from Australia, are widespread in the Mediterranean region. *Acacia dealbata**, the florist's mimosa, is popular in the South of France, where it grows as a small- to medium-sized tree; it is called silver wattle in its homeland because the attractive, deeply divided young leaves are covered with a silvery down. It is also covered with fragrant flowers in early spring. Hard frost is likely to kill it. *A. retinodes FT* is also widely cultivated, and has long, linear leaves. *A. longifolia* has willow-like leaves and bright yellow flowers. All varieties grow well in containers, and as shrubs in the garden, but they may need winter protection.

ARBUTUS UNEDO ***
A handsome evergreen *maquis* bush or tree with red bark and red-edged, lime green glossy leaves, which grow towards the sky in clusters. White bellflowers appear at the same time as the strawberry-like fruits in autumn. *Unedo* means "I eat one", meaning that if you taste one fruit, you won't want any more. Tolerant of sea gales, the arbutus can reach 10m/33ft after many years.

CERCIS SILIQUASTRUM ***
The Judas tree is supposedly the tree upon which Judas Iscariot hanged himself, causing it to blush with shame, hence the beautiful purplish-pink pea flowers in late spring that cover the tree. These are followed by smooth, heart-shaped leaves and red seed pods. A native of the Mediterranean, especially Spain and Portugal, the Judas tree is hardy, but needs a warm, sunny spot to put on its best show and resents being moved. Its ultimate height and spread are around 8m/26ft.

CHAMAEROPS HUMILIS *
The dwarf fan palm is a *garrigue* native that forms a mass of stiff foliage fans in dark green or sometimes even smoky blue. The growing tips are sometimes eaten, and the leaf fibres are used for rope. The fan palm makes a striking architectural plant that can reach 2–3m/6–10ft in height, and eventually suckers to make a broad, bushy plant. It will survive only in a mild location, so the answer for most of us is to grow *Chamaerops humilis* in a large terracotta container, where it looks splendid. Feed and water well in summer. Large specimens are more likely to tolerate a few degrees of frost.

CUPRESSUS SEMPERVIRENS ***
The elegant green column of the Italian cypress transforms the landscape and adds instant Mediterranean status to a garden. Suitably streamlined forms such as 'Stricta' are available from nurseries as container-grown plants, but they should be bought small, because they dislike being transplanted. Severe winters can damage them.

ERICA ARBOREA **
The tree heath grows on acid soils in evergreen Mediterranean woods, and can reach 3m/10ft in height and spread. If you can supply the right soil and adequate space, the tree heath is a stunning sight in spring and summer, when the dense branches of evergreen needle-like leaves are covered in clusters of small white bellflowers.

GENISTA AETNENSIS **
The Mount Etna broom from Sicily and Sardinia is easy to grow from seed, if you have the patience to wait a few years for it to make a height of approx 4m/13ft or more. With its graceful, spreading dome of rush-like branches, *Genista aetnensis* looks spectacular in the right spot, especially when studded with flowers in late summer. The bonus of growing this small tree is that the airy, nearly leafless branches cast virtually no shade, so you can use the space beneath to grow sun-loving plants.

Acacia longifolia.

Arbutus unedo.

Cercis siliquastrum.

Chamaerops humilis.

Cupressus sempervirens.

Juniperus communis.

Phoenix canariensis.

Pinus pinaster.

JUNIPERUS COMMUNIS ***

Is it a tree? Is it a shrub? Obligingly the fragrant juniper can be either, making a low, sprawling, evergreen shrub, a tall, upright tree and a million shapes in between to consider for your garden.

Left to its own devices, common juniper will form a dense shrub that will eventually reach 5m/16ft. *Juniperus communis* 'Compressa' makes a vertical shape that emulates Italian cypresses but reaches only 1m/39in, while 'Sentinel' is more slender, making it perfect to plant between mounded evergreen shrubs. If the branches splay out, which is a tendency with 'Sentinel', secure them into the framework with garden twine.

PHOENIX CANARIENSIS FT

The Canary Island date palm is widely planted in the Mediterranean as a decorative tree, but it is not one for the small garden. The date palm can be grown as a handsome container plant to fulfil many a gardener's dream of owning the classic palm tree, but don't hold your breath for bunches of dates. It can reach 15m/50ft when grown in a warm garden, though it is usually much less, and it has a broad trunk.

PINUS ***

Pine trees are an important part of the Mediterranean landscape, notably the conical Aleppo pine, *Pinus halepensis*, the familiar umbrella pine, *Pinus pinea*, and the tall, pyramidal maritime pine, *Pinus pinaster*.

The ancient Greeks collected resin from the bark of the Aleppo pine to flavour and preserve the local wine, and today, over 3,000 tons of resin from the same species are still used in the manufacture of the traditional Greek wine, retsina.

A pine tree may not be a practical proposition in your garden – the three Mediterranean species grow to a maximum of about 20m/65ft – but you could replace the larger species with a smaller one such as the dwarf mountain pine *Pinus mugo*, which makes a good tactile contrast to velvety grey *maquis* plants.

PRUNUS CERASUS 'MORELLO' ***

Invaluable because it grows happily on a sunless wall, the Morello cherry produces white spring blossom followed by acid cherries that make the most delicious jam.

A second advantage is that it does not need another tree for pollination. The Morello cherry is especially suited to fan-training, but wherever the site give it a sheltered spot that is not in a frost pocket. Be sure to buy a tree with the appropriate rootstock for the size of your garden, and incorporate fertilizer when planting.

PUNICA GRANATUM **

Even if you cannot grow the fruits with their exotic pulp, the pomegranate is a delectable ornamental tree with outstanding deciduous foliage of dainty, lime green glossy leaves that grow increasingly flushed with red as summer progresses. In late summer, paper-like vermilion flowers grow from thick, waxy calyxes. In the variety *Punica granatum* f. *plena*, these are double-flowered.

The pomegranate has ancient and mystical connections and is often mentioned in the Bible; although of Asian origin, it has naturalized in the Mediterranean and is widely grown in gardens. It can grow to a maximum height of 6m/20ft, but it usually grows less than this. *Punica granatum* var. *nana* is a dwarf, shrubby pomegranate that is ideal for containers.

TAMARIX see pages 66–7.

TRACHYCARPUS FORTUNEI **

The Chusan palm is the hardiest palm for cooler climates, and can survive frost, but it still needs a sheltered site such as a city microclimate in order to thrive. The leaves look like large, spiny fans, and, although they are tough they can be damaged by winds; the trunk is covered with matted fibres from the sheaths of the old leaves. The Chusan palm can reach 12m/40ft when grown in the ground.

Prunus cerasus 'Morello'.

Punica granatum f. plena.

Trachycarpus fortunei.

Sources and acknowledgements

UK Plants

The Vernon Geranium Nursery, Cuddington Way, Cheam, Sutton, Surrey SM2 7JB; (0181) 393 7616
Geranium collections

Jekka's Herb Farm, Rose Cottage, Shellards Lane, Alveston, Bristol BS12 2SY; (01454) 418878
Organic herbs and olive trees

Jacques Amand, The Nurseries, Clamp Hill, Stanmore, Middlesex HA7 3JS; (0181) 427 3968
Variety of bulbs

Avon Bulbs, Burnt House Farm, Mid Lambrook, South Petherton, Somerset TA13 5HE; (01460) 242177
Variety of bulbs

Unusual Plants, The Beth Chatto Gardens, Elmstead Market, Colchester CO7 7DB; (01206) 822007
Large variety of perennials, grasses

Burncoose & Southdown, Gwennap, Redruth, Cornwall TR16 6BJ; (01209) 861112
Shrubs, trees and conservatory plants

The Citrus Centre, Marehill Nursery, West Mare Lane, Pulborough, West Sussex RH20 2EA; (01798) 872786
Variety of citrus plants

The Mead Nursery, Brokerswood, nr Westbury, Wiltshire, BA13 4EG; (01373) 859990
Perennials, alpines and dwarf bulbs

UK Seeds

Chiltern Seeds, Bortree Stile, Ulverston, Cumbria LA12 7PB; (01229) 581137

Suffolk Herbs, Monks Farm, Coggeshall Road, Kelvedon, Essex CO5 9PG; (01376) 572456

Thompson & Morgan, Poplar Lane, Ipswich, Suffolk, IP8 3BU; (01473) 688821

US Plants

Digging Dog Nursery, 31101 Middle Ridge Road, Albion, CA 95410; (707) 937-1130

Goodwin Creek Gardens, PO Box 83, Williams, OR 97544; (541) 846-7357

Heronswood Nursery Ltd., 7530 N.E. 288h, Kingston, WA 98346

Plant Delights Nursery, Inc., 9241 Sauls Road, Raleigh, NC 27603; (919) 772-4794

Yucca Do Nursery, PO Box 450, Waller, TX 77484

Australian Plants

Nursery Industry Association, Swanes, 490 Galston Road, Dural NSW 2158; 02 9651 1322

Sherringhames Nursery Pty Ltd, 299a Land Cove Road, North Ryde, NSW 2113; 02 9888 3133

Nursery Industry Association, The Greenery, 4 Banksia St, Heidelberg VIC 3084; 03 9459 8433

Garden World, 810 Springvale Road, Keysbourgh VIC 3173; 03 9798 8095

Nursery Industry Association, Heyne's Nurseries Pty Ltd, 287–287 The Parade, Beulah Park SA 5067; 08 8332 2933

Peter Keelan's Garden Centre, 129–133 Brighton Road, Glenelg South SA 5045; 08 8295 4874

Nursery Industry Association,
Gardenway Nurseries,
269 Monier Road, Darra QLD 4076;
07 279 3100

Materials

Mosaic
Romantique Mosiac Centre,
12 Pulteney Bridge, Bath BA2 4AY;
(01225) 463073
Free price list of mosaic available

Tile Paints
Porcelaine 150 in 47 colours, by
Pebeo, from all good artists' suppliers

Terracotta Pots
Whichford Pottery, Whichford,
nr Shipston on Stour, Warwickshire,
CV36 5PG; (01608) 685516
Distinctive hand-made
terracotta pots

Landscape Materials
Reconstituted stone in blocks
used in pond wall and plinth
construction from Bradstone Garden
Landscaping, ring (01335) 372289
for nearest suppliers

Acknowledgements

The publishers and author are
grateful to the following people for
giving us permission to feature their
gardens in this book:

Mike Nelhams, curator, The Abbey
Gardens, Tresco, Scilly Isles
Jim Buckland and **Sarah Wain**,
West Dean Gardens, Chichester,
West Sussex

Beth Chatto, The Beth Chatto
Gardens, Elmstead Market,
Colchester, Essex
Fiona Lawrenson's Provence garden
at Chelsea Flower show 1997
Don Leevers and **Lindsay
Megarrity**, Venzano, Volterra, Italy
Jekka McVicar, Jekka's Herb Farm,
Alveston, Bristol
Steve and Emma Lewis-Dale, The
Mead Nursery, Westbury, Wiltshire

Photograph acknowledgements

The publishers are grateful to the
following photographers and organiz-
ations for giving us permission to
feature their photographs in this book:

A–Z Botanical: 67tr, 86br, 97tr,
146bmr, 151br, 153tr, 155tmr.
Garden Picture Library: 67bl,
151bmr, 152bmr, 154bl.
Garden & Wildlife Matters: 62bm,
62br, 66bl, 67br, 72t, 149tml.
Bob Gibbons, Natural Image: 6,
12, 14both, 15all, 56br, 63bl, 101br,
148bml, 149tl, 155tml, 155tr, 155bl.
John Glover: 72br, 75br, 76tr, 76br,
149bmr, 150bmr, 154bml, 155br
The Image Bank: 128tl.
Andrew Lawson: 153bl.
Vivian Russell: 8bl, 9tr, 96, 111 all,
155tl
Elizabeth Whiting Associates:
76tm, 148tr.

Key
t = top, b = bottom, m = middle,
l = left, r = right

Author's acknowledgements

My thanks:
To Norman Barron, for his painting
skills; Phyllis Barron, for her shell
artistry; Claire Benison, for designing
the central panel in the Moroccan
mosaic table; Bradstone, for their
landscaping stone that has made such
a difference to my garden; Dave
Evans, for his contributions to both
gardens; Alison Hughes, for her
constant ferrying and smiles; Steve
Lewis-Dale, for sharing his trough-
making techniques, for his creative
input on the island bed and for the
superb plants from his nursery, The
Mead Nursery; Richard Mabey, for
his knowlege on Mediterranean
plants, support and encouragement;
Simon McBride, for his beautiful
pictures, infinite patience and input
on Italian gardens; Deirdre McSharry,
for her constant encouragement and
glamorous garden chairs; Jekka
McVicar, for her terrific herbs that
have been the mainstay of my garden,
and for sharing her knowledge on
herb growing and propagating; Brian
Mears, for his practical and expert
advice; Frances Mears, for being the
perfect hand model; Colin Stokes, for
building such beautiful garden walls
and terraces; Virginia Stokes, for her
invaluable spadework; Sarah Wain for
her beautiful chilli peppers.

reference

Index